THE BANK PROMOTION INTERVIEW SECRETS

27 INSIDER-STYLE MOCK INTERVIEWS THAT SIMULATE REAL PANELS & UNLOCK YOUR NEXT PROMOTION

KUMAR GAURAV KHULLAR

Made with ♥ on the Notion Press Platform
www.notionpress.com

To my beloved mother, Smt. Punam, whose strength and unwavering love shaped my destiny.Single-handedly, she nurtured and educated me after losing my father when I was barely two, becoming my greatest inspiration and role model.

To my dear wife, whose unwavering faith gave me the strength to step away from the comfort of a 9-to-5 life and pursue my true calling in Writing, Teaching, and Research in the field of Banking. This journey wouldn't have been possible without your constant support and belief in me.

And my wonderful daughters, Pavi and Udyati, whose laughter and endless joy fuel my soul. You are my constant motivation and my sanctuary amidst life's pressures.

This book is for you.

Contents

Contents

Contents

Preface

Every banker has a moment—when the panel door closes behind you, and the real test begins.

It's not a test of your memory. It's a test of your clarity, your calm, and your character. It's where theory fades, and real banking begins.

I've sat across the table as a banker, I've stood outside it as a mentor, and I've seen too many promising professionals walk in with potential—but walk out without promotion.

This book was born from that pain. And that promise.

I've worked in cash-heavy rural branches, fought compliance battles in urban settings, and handled crisis where circulars offered no help. But the greatest insight came after I stepped out of the system. When I began teaching, listening, and mentoring thousands of bankers preparing for the same interviews that once defined me—I realized something:

We're over-trained on answers. And under-trained on awareness.

Promotion is no longer about rehearsed answers—it's about how you process complexity, carry composure, and reflect readiness. It's about transforming your everyday firefighting—be it managing a cash mismatch, resolving a viral social media complaint, or tackling overdue KCC loans—into structured, boardroom-worthy leadership. It's about explaining a cyber fraud recovery without panic, navigating ₹500 crore loan decisions with sharp risk clarity, or responding to a politically sensitive NPA with balanced judgment. Sometimes, it's even about owning your setbacks—whether it's a past suspension or a flawed answer—and turning them into proof of growth, maturity, and grace under pressure.

What you're holding is not a simple collection of mock interviews. It's a mirror, a mentor, and in many ways, a mindset manual.

Each mock interview inside is based on real journeys—from clerks to chief managers. Some candidates fought language gaps. Others rose after suspensions. Some cracked forex with no treasury experience. Others turned rural adversity into boardroom clarity. What unites them is not perfection—but preparation, self-awareness, and the ability to lead with authenticity.

This book took months to curate—not just writing and rewriting, but listening to real interview experiences of bankers, decoding panel psychology, and crafting role-specific scenarios from Clerk to AGM level promotion interviews. Every question is placed with a purpose. Every response is built to stretch your thinking—not just your memory.

This book is not a shortcut. It's a shift.

If you're holding this, you're serious. About your next role. About your growth. About banking that goes beyond transactions.

So whether you're a Scale I officer bracing for a treasury cross-question or a Clerk who's never touched a loan file—**this book is your edge.** Not because it gives you answers, but because it trains you to think, reflect, and rise.

Lastly, don't just read these interviews—feel them. Learn from their errors. Borrow their structure. And most importantly, use them as a mirror to sharpen your own edge.

The panel room is not just a place of judgment. It's the gateway to impact.

Let's walk in ready.

Kumar Gaurav Khullar
Banking Coach | Mentor to 67,000+ Bankers
kumargauravkhullar1@gmail.com
+91-7830481000 (Whatsapp)

How To Proceed With This Book?

Congratulations on embarking upon this insightful journey, one designed specifically to enrich your knowledge, sharpen your decision-making skills, and enhance your practical banking acumen. Before you begin exploring the compelling scenarios and mock interviews laid out in the following chapters, allow me to share with you the optimal approach to deriving maximum benefit from this book.

Universal Relevance of Interviews

You are strongly advised to go through all the interviews in this book, irrespective of the scale for which you are preparing. Whether you're a clerical staff aiming for Scale I or an officer aspiring for promotion to Scale II, III, IV or even V, the interview questions presented are relevant across the board.

While the type of questions remains similar across different scales, what varies is the depth, articulation, and maturity of the answers expected by the panel. So even if you're targeting Scale II to III, reviewing Scale IV to V interviews will expose you to higher-order thinking and response framing.

Please do not get intimidated by interviews labeled for higher scales. Each has been designed to build your strategic thinking and situational judgment, traits that are universally expected in any interview panel.

Educational and Hypothetical Nature

All interviews featured in this book are hypothetical in nature, carefully crafted for educational purposes. Names of individuals, banks, places, and branches are purely fictional. They have been introduced solely to create relatable and immersive learning environments. Any resemblance to real entities is purely coincidental.

Emphasis on Scenario-Based Learning

Each interview presents real-life-like situations a banker might face during daily operations or decision-making moments. Your focus should not just be on memorizing questions and answers but on understanding the underlying thought process, strategy, and compliance logic applied by the candidate.

During your real interview, the panel may present similar scenarios and seek your response to judge your handling ability, ethical grounding, and understanding of internal guidelines.

While this book provides a generic framework, you must link your replies in actual interviews to your bank-specific circulars, policies, and product offerings. Personalizing your answers with real-time, bank-specific data adds both authenticity and accuracy.

A Structured Approach to Maximize Value

To get the most from this book, adopt the following structured approach:
1) Active Reading: Place yourself mentally in each interviewee's position. Ask yourself, "How would I respond to this question or scenario?" This active participation will elevate your learning manifold.
2) Critical Thinking and Analysis: You are encouraged to analyze each question and the candidate's response critically. Ask yourself, was the response complete, clear, and confident? How would you have responded differently? Such self-reflection will help you identify areas of improvement, sharpen your articulation, and deepen your understanding of what the interview panel expects.
3) Scenario Analysis: Don't just look at the questions, analyze the entire scenario: how the panel asks follow-up questions, how the candidate builds his response, and how clarity and confidence are maintained throughout.
4) Discussion and Debate: Share interviews with peers or colleagues. Discuss possible alternative responses, mistakes made, or better phrasing of replies. These group discussions often open up fresh perspectives.
5) Continuous Learning: Pay extra attention to interviews that deal with compliance lapses, audit remarks, risk assessment, grievance redressal, or digital frauds, these are increasingly common areas of focus in actual panels.

Final Thought

This book goes beyond theory. It is designed to shape your practical judgment, presence of mind, and ethical response system, skills that will serve you not only during the interview but throughout your banking career.

Approach this book with curiosity, humility, and a commitment to self-improvement. Learn from every page, unlearn outdated practices, and relearn smarter, sharper approaches.

Let's begin this transformative journey together!

CHAPTER I

Clerk No More: How Balwant Combines Ethics, Insight, and Readiness for the Next Role?

Interview Snapshot - (Clerical to Scale I)
What happens when eight years of grassroots banking meet tough leadership scenarios? This interview with Balwant Govindrao Lokhande is a case study in composure, ethics, and customer-centric thinking. From managing cash mismatches and illiterate account holders to detecting suspicious transactions and responding to liquidity crises, his responses reflect readiness for the officer's chair. If you're aiming to step up from clerk to Scale 1, this mock interview will show you how to blend operational awareness with problem-solving finesse and ethical judgment.

Candidate Profile - Balwant Govindrao Lokhande (Clerk)
Balwant Govindrao Lokhande, a dedicated banking professional from Solapur, Maharashtra, has been serving in Latur(Rural Region) for the past 8 years as a Clerk. His responsibilities include cash handling, account opening, and signature scanning, where he has consistently delivered accuracy and efficiency. A Certified Associate of the Indian Institute of Bankers (CAIIB), Balwant has been recognized twice as "Employee of the Quarter" for his exceptional customer service and ability to manage high-volume transactions. With a strong problem-solving mindset and frontline experience, he aspires to transition into a Scale 1 Officer role to embrace greater leadership and operational responsibilities.

$$\bullet \ \bullet \ \bullet$$

Interviewer: "Good morning, Mr. Lokhande. Congratulations on being shortlisted for the Scale 1 Officer interview. How are you feeling today?"

Balwant Govindrao Lokhande: "Good morning, Sir. Thank you so much! I feel honored to be here and am looking forward to this opportunity."

Interviewer: "That's great to hear. I see you've been serving as a clerk in Latur(Rural Region) for eight years now. Solapur is your hometown, isn't it? How has the transition from Solapur to Latur been for you, personally and professionally?"

Lokhande: "Yes, Sir, that's correct. The transition was challenging initially since I had to adapt to a new environment. But Latur to Solapur is not that far. Culturally both are similar. Infact, Latur has been a rewarding experience for me. The rural banking exposure has taught me the basics of customer service, especially when it comes to serving diverse socio-economic groups."

Interviewer:[*nodding thoughtfully*] "Interesting. Given your customer-facing role, I'd like to ask: Can you recall a time when you faced a cash difference or mismatch? How did you handle the situation?"

Lokhande: "Certainly, Sir. There was an instance during a particularly busy day when I discovered a cash mismatch of ₹ 9,000 during the end-of-day balancing. I immediately stopped all non-essential activities and started a thorough rechecking of transaction records and physical cash. I cross-verified vouchers, withdrawal slips, and deposit receipts along with my colleagues, paying special attention to high-value transactions. Ultimately, I identified a voucher entry that had been incorrectly posted. I incorrectly posted a ₹1000 voucher as ₹10,000. I then corrected the error and ensured that the day's balance tallied. To prevent recurrence, I introduced a practice of mid-day balancing during peak periods, which has significantly reduced errors since then."

Interviewer:[*smiling slightly*] "Well done, Balwant. Resolving such issues calmly and methodically is crucial in banking operations. Let's move on to the next question."

Interviewer: "Now, moving on to an operational question. As you may know, opening accounts for illiterate persons is a unique challenge. Can you explain the process for opening such accounts, based on your experience?"

Lokhande: "Yes, Sir. For illiterate persons, a savings account can be opened provided they bring a recent passport-sized photograph. Their thumb impression or mark is taken on the account opening form in the presence of a bank official. This thumb impression is equivalent to their signature. However, current accounts cannot be opened for illiterate persons as per the norms. Additionally, we ensure they are well-informed about their account usage to prevent fraud."

Interviewer: "Excellent explanation. Since you're well-versed with rural banking, tell me, how would you ensure strict control over Non-Performing Assets (NPAs) at your branch, especially in the agriculture segment?"

Lokhande: "Sir, controlling NPAs in the agriculture segment requires timely intervention. First, I'd ensure periodic reviews and renewals of loan accounts to identify potential defaults early. Second, I'd focus on a personal approach by involving village influencers like gram pradhans during recovery processes. Finally, I'd leverage recovery tools like the SARFAESI Act for non agriculture land and collaborate with Debt Recovery Tribunals if needed, while also offering rehabilitation options for genuine cases."

Interviewer:[*smiling*] "That's a comprehensive plan. Speaking of rural banking, let's discuss priority sector lending. Can you identify some borrower categories under weaker sections, as per RBI guidelines?"

Lokhande: "Certainly, Sir. Weaker section borrowers include small and marginal farmers, artisans and village industries with credit limits up to

₹1 lakh, beneficiaries under schemes like NRLM and NULM, Scheduled Castes and Tribes, beneficiaries of the Differential Rate of Interest scheme, Self Help Groups, and distressed farmers indebted to non-institutional lenders."

Interviewer: "You're well-prepared. Let's move to a hypothetical scenario now. Suppose your branch manager is on leave, and you notice a sharp increase in cash deposits from a particular account holder across multiple branches in the district. How would you handle this situation?"

Lokhande: "Sir, such behavior could indicate structuring or money laundering. I'd immediately flag the transactions as suspicious under the guidelines of the Prevention of Money Laundering Act (PMLA). Simultaneously, I'd report the matter to the Compliance Officer and guide the team to conduct enhanced due diligence on the customer. Ensuring the bank's compliance with AML norms would be my priority."

Interviewer: "That's the kind of vigilance we need in today's banking environment. One important question, Balwant. Open Banking has been a transformative concept in the financial sector, but it's not without its challenges. Can you elaborate on the demerits of Open Banking?"

Lokhande: "Certainly, Sir. While Open Banking enhances innovation and customer-centric solutions, it does have some notable demerits. First, there are significant concerns regarding data security and privacy, as sharing financial data with third-party service providers increases the risk of breaches. Second, smaller banks may struggle to keep up with the technological advancements required for Open Banking, leading to a potential imbalance in competition. Third, customers who are less tech-savvy might face difficulties in understanding and using Open Banking services, which could lead to financial exclusion for certain sections of society. Lastly, regulatory oversight can be challenging, as ensuring compliance across multiple stakeholders adds complexity."

Interviewer:[*nodding with interest*] "A well-rounded answer, Balwant. It's clear you've thought about both the opportunities and challenges of this evolving concept. "

Interviewer: "Balwant, let's delve into some challenging scenarios. Your branch has been given an aggressive target to sell insurance and investment products. However, several staff members are selling these products to customers who lack financial literacy, sometimes misrepresenting the features. How will you address this issue while achieving targets ethically?"

Lokhande: "Sir, this is a delicate situation requiring a balanced approach. I would first organize training sessions for staff to emphasize ethical selling practices and ensure they fully understand the products. Then, I'd establish a process to profile customers' financial literacy and needs before suggesting products. To prevent misrepresentation, I'd monitor sales closely, encourage transparency, and communicate to customers in simple terms. Lastly, I'd aim to create awareness among customers about their rights, ensuring they make informed decisions. By focusing on building trust, I believe both customer satisfaction and targets can be achieved."

Interviewer:[*nodding approvingly*] "That's a very thoughtful strategy, Balwant. Now, let's consider another challenging scenario. Your branch experiences a sudden liquidity crunch due to large withdrawals by depositors. The head office asks you to manage the situation without seeking immediate external funding. How would you approach this?"

Lokhande: "Sir, in such a situation, my priority would be to maintain depositor confidence and ensure operational continuity. I'd first evaluate the branch's liquidity position and prioritize critical payments. Next, I'd promote alternate banking channels like ATMs, digital platforms, and UPI to reduce cash dependency. I'd also coordinate with nearby branches to explore options for transferring surplus cash. Communicating proactively with customers, explaining the measures being taken, and setting realistic timelines for fulfilling their needs would be critical to regaining trust. Internally, I'd initiate discussions with staff to handle the situation calmly and efficiently."

Interviewer: "Practical and well-rounded approach. Now, let's discuss a credit-related issue. Suppose a customer applies for a business loan of ₹1 crore, offering land as collateral. Upon verification, you find that the land is under litigation. How would you handle this case, ensuring compliance with bank policies and maintaining a balance between customer service and risk management?"

Lokhande: "Sir, as per bank policies, accepting collateral under litigation poses a significant risk. I'd inform the customer about the issue and explain why the collateral cannot be accepted in its current status. I'd then explore alternative options with the customer, such as providing additional collateral, a co-borrower with a strong credit profile, or restructuring the loan amount to mitigate risk. Throughout the process, I'd ensure that communication remains empathetic and transparent, fostering a positive relationship with the customer while adhering to compliance norms."

Interviewer:*[smiling and leaning back]* "Balwant, your responses reflect a deep understanding of banking operations and a strong sense of ethics and customer-centricity. I must say, you've performed admirably today, showing confidence and clarity in every response. Do you have any questions for us before we conclude?"

Lokhande:*[with a polite smile]* "Thank you, Sir. I just wanted to understand how Scale 1 Officers are trained to take on leadership responsibilities, particularly in handling complex operational challenges?"

Interviewer: "That's a great question. In our bank, Scale 1 Officers undergo rigorous on-the-job training and attend specialized workshops designed to enhance their managerial and operational skills. They are also mentored by senior officers to help them adapt to leadership roles effectively. It's a challenging yet highly rewarding journey."

Interviewer:*[standing up and extending a hand]* "Thank you, Balwant. You've done an excellent job, and I wish you the very best for the next stages of the promotion process."

Lokhande:*[shaking hands with a confident smile]* "Thank you so much, Sir. It was an honor to interact with you. I'll strive to meet the expectations of the bank."

• • •

CHAPTER II

Leading Under Pressure: How Shibu Balanced Profit, NPAs, and Political Influence on his Journey to Scale 3

Interview Snapshot- (Scale II to III)
This mock interview offers a masterclass in leadership, strategic thinking, and ethical decision-making. Shibu C George shares how he turned around a struggling rural branch while confronting rising NPAs, political pressure, and digital adoption challenges. His answers reflect a deep understanding of MSME norms, factoring vs. forfaiting, CIBIL benchmarks, and practical solutions to real-world issues like PSL shortfalls and connectivity gaps. A must-read for anyone looking to craft balanced, well-reasoned responses that demonstrate both managerial capability and grassroots-level sensitivity.

Candidate Profile - Shibu C George (Manager, Scale II)
Shibu C George, a dedicated banker with 10 years of experience, hails from Kottayam, Kerala, and is currently posted as a Scale II Officer in Salem, Tamil Nadu. As the Branch Manager of a rural branch in Thondamuthur, he successfully turned a loss-making unit into a profit-generating one, showcasing strong business acumen. However, the journey also saw a 25% rise in NPAs, reflecting the complexity of growth in rural credit. A certified Risk Management Professional, Shibu aspires for an overseas posting after promotion to Scale III, aiming to expand his global exposure in banking operations

• • •

Interviewer: "Good morning, Mr. Shibu C George. Congratulations on being shortlisted for your Scale 3 promotion interview. How are you feeling about this next step in your career?"

Shibu: "Good morning, Sir. Thank you so much. I am feeling excited and confident. It's been a journey filled with challenges and learnings, and I'm eager to take on greater responsibilities."

Interviewer: "That's the spirit, Mr. George. I see you hail from Kottayam in Kerala but are currently posted in Thondamuthur, Tamil Nadu. How has the transition to a different state and culture been for you?"

Shibu: "Sir, the transition was initially challenging, especially with language barriers and cultural differences. However, I took it as an opportunity to learn and adapt. Interacting with the locals and understanding their needs has been both fulfilling and insightful."

Interviewer:[*nodding*] "Adapting to a new environment while managing a rural branch is commendable. Speaking of your rural branch, I noticed you successfully converted it from a loss-making branch to a profit-making one. Can you elaborate on the strategies you implemented?"

Shibu: "Certainly, Sir. When I took charge, I observed that the branch had untapped potential in agricultural and MSME financing. I focused on financial inclusion by promoting KCCs and SHG loans. Simultaneously, I encouraged cross-selling of third-party products like insurance to enhance fee-based income. We also strengthened our deposit base through local engagement initiatives. These efforts, combined with streamlining internal operations, contributed to our turnaround."

Interviewer:[*leaning forward*] "Impressive work. However, I noticed the NPAs rose by 25% during the same period. What do you think caused this, and what is your plan to curtail it?"

Shibu: "Sir, the rise in NPAs was partly due to negligence of my previous branch head and partly due to the impact of the pandemic on borrowers' repayment capacity. To address this, I plan to intensify recovery efforts through regular follow-ups and settlement camps. I also intend to strengthen pre-sanction appraisal processes and ensure timely credit monitoring to prevent slippages."

Interviewer:[*smiling*] "That sounds like a balanced approach. Now, let's move to MSME classifications. Could you explain the investment and turnover thresholds for micro, small, and medium enterprises as per the latest guidelines?"

Shibu: "Certainly, Sir. As per the updated classification:

For Micro Enterprises: Investment in plant and machinery or equipment is up to ₹2.5 crore and annual turnover is up to ₹10 crore.

For Small Enterprises: Investment is up to ₹25 crore and turnover is up to ₹100 crore.

Lastly for, Medium Enterprises: Investment is up to ₹125 crore and turnover is up to ₹500 crore."

Interviewer:[*raising an eyebrow*] "Spot on. Let's move to another interesting area—factoring and forfaiting. Can you differentiate between the two?"

Shibu: "Sure, Sir. Factoring involves financing up to 75-80% of the invoice value, while forfaiting provides 100% financing of the invoice value. In factoring, the factor evaluates the creditworthiness of the debtor, whereas forfaiting banks rely on the credibility of the availing bank. Factoring includes services like sales administration, whereas forfaiting does not offer such services. Additionally, factoring can be with or without recourse, whereas forfaiting is always without recourse."

Interviewer:[*smiling approvingly*] "You've explained that well. Now, since you handle a branch, CIBIL scores must play a critical role in loan sanctions. What is the ideal CIBIL score you use as a benchmark for approving loans?"

Shibu: "Sir, while the ideal CIBIL score is 750 and above, we consider profiles with scores between 700 and 750 based on additional risk mitigants like co-applicants or collateral. However, anything below 700 requires a thorough evaluation."

Interviewer: "Good to know. Now let's test your decision-making with a hypothetical scenario. Suppose a borrower in your branch defaults on a ₹25 lakh MSME loan due to unforeseen business losses. The borrower approaches you with a request for restructuring. How would you handle this?"

Shibu: "Sir, I would first assess the borrower's repayment history and the reason for default. If it's a genuine case of business distress, I would follow RBI guidelines on restructuring MSME loans. This could include extending the loan tenure or offering a moratorium period. I would ensure the borrower demonstrates a viable revival plan before proceeding with restructuring."

Interviewer:[*nodding thoughtfully*] "Practical and aligned with regulatory norms. Since you've expressed interest in an overseas posting, let's touch upon global banking trends. How do you see digital currencies impacting traditional banking systems in the future?"

Shibu: "Digital currencies, especially Central Bank Digital Currencies (CBDCs), have the potential to complement traditional banking by enhancing transparency and reducing transaction costs. However, they also pose challenges like cybersecurity risks and regulatory uncertainties. Banks must adapt by investing in technology and collaborating with fintechs to remain relevant."

Interviewer:[*leaning back*] "Interesting perspective. Finally, one last question to test your resilience. Suppose you are promoted and posted in a branch with connectivity issues where customers grow increasingly agitated due to delayed services. How would you handle the situation?"

Shibu: "Sir, in such a situation, I would ensure open communication with customers to manage expectations. I would also deploy alternate arrangements, such as connecting with a nearby branch or using mobile banking vans. Additionally, I would escalate the connectivity issue to higher authorities for a long-term resolution."

Interviewer: "Alright, Mr. George, let's continue with a few more scenarios to further gauge your approach and expertise. Here's the first one: The bank has set a target to migrate 60% of branch-based transactions to digital channels within six months. You are responsible for a branch where the majority of customers are senior citizens and small business owners. How will you achieve this target while ensuring customer satisfaction and smooth service delivery?"

Shibu: "Sir, this is a challenging yet achievable target. My strategy would revolve around a phased and inclusive approach. First, I would segment our customers into groups based on their digital literacy levels. For senior citizens, I would organize weekly workshops at the branch to demonstrate the use of digital banking apps, UPI platforms, and net banking. These workshops would include hands-on practice sessions and step-by-step guides in their local language to make them comfortable with the technology.

For small business owners, I would highlight the benefits of digital banking, such as reduced transaction time, better tracking of payments, and lower transaction costs. I would visit their premises and conduct personalized demonstrations of POS machines, payment gateways, and bulk payment tools. Incentives like waivers on digital transaction fees for the first six months could motivate them further.

Additionally, I would deploy branch staff as digital ambassadors to assist customers in real-time whenever they face issues with digital channels. To ensure smooth service delivery, I would set up a dedicated helpline and escalate recurring technical issues to the IT team promptly. Regular monitoring and feedback from customers would help fine-tune our efforts and ensure their satisfaction during this transition."

Interviewer:[*nodding appreciatively*] "That's a comprehensive approach, Mr. George. Let's move to another critical area. Your branch has not met its Priority Sector Lending (PSL) targets for the past two quarters. The regional office has directed immediate action. Suggest a strategy to meet PSL requirements while adhering to risk assessment norms and maintaining asset quality."

Shibu: "Sir, meeting PSL targets requires a mix of aggressive outreach and cautious lending. My first step would be to analyze the branch's existing PSL portfolio and identify the segments where we are falling short, such as agriculture, MSMEs, or weaker sections. I would then conduct outreach programs in partnership with local self-help groups, NGOs, and community leaders to identify eligible borrowers.

For agriculture, I would promote products like Kisan Credit Cards and crop loans by collaborating with the local agriculture department and attending farmer fairs. For MSMEs, I would organize financial literacy camps to educate small business owners about government schemes like CGTMSE and Mudra loans.

To maintain asset quality, I would strengthen pre-sanction due diligence by thoroughly assessing borrowers' repayment capacity and business viability. Setting up a PSL task force within the branch, including credit officers and field staff, would ensure targeted efforts and timely disbursals. Continuous monitoring of sanctioned loans would minimize slippages and help maintain a healthy PSL portfolio."

Interviewer:[*leaning forward*] "Excellent strategy. Now for a more sensitive situation: A local politician pressures you to sanction a large agricultural loan for a group of farmers without adequate collateral. How would you handle this situation, ensuring adherence to the bank's credit policies and maintaining the branch's reputation?"

Shibu: "Sir, such situations require tact and firmness to uphold the bank's credit policies without compromising relationships. I would first acknowledge the politician's concerns and express my willingness to support the farmers within the framework of the bank's guidelines.

I would explain that agricultural loans are assessed based on various factors, including creditworthiness, repayment capacity, and collateral, to ensure the sustainability of both the borrower and the bank. If the farmers meet these criteria, I would gladly expedite the loan process. However, if they do not, I would politely but firmly communicate that granting loans without proper evaluation could lead to defaults, which would harm the farmers' long-term financial prospects and the branch's reputation.

To avoid escalating tensions, I would offer alternative solutions, such as encouraging the farmers to apply under government subsidy or guarantee schemes, which could offset the need for collateral. Simultaneously, I would involve my regional office to keep them informed about the situation and seek their guidance if needed. Maintaining transparency and adhering to ethical practices would be my priority while handling such pressure."

Interviewer: *[smiling]* "That's an admirable stance, Mr. George. Balancing diplomacy with principles is critical in our profession. I must say, your responses have been thoughtful and well-articulated throughout this conversation. Let's conclude here for today. Thank you for your time and insights."

Shibu: "Thank you, Sir. It was a privilege to interact with you and share my thoughts. I look forward to further opportunities to contribute to the bank's growth."

Interviewer:*[standing up]* "Likewise, Mr. George. I wish you all the best for your promotion. Keep up the excellent work."

• • •

CHAPTER III

Suspended TWICE? This Banker's Shocking Past Nearly Cost him his Promotion: Until he Fought Back!

Interview Snapshot - (Scale I to II)

This interview is an emotional roller coaster that dives straight into the fire—suspensions, bluntness, behavioral red flags—and yet emerges with powerful redemption. Micheal MJ faces brutal questioning not only on his past but on his temperament, leadership readiness, and risk-taking ability. But it's how he owns his flaws, defends his transformation, and delivers razor-sharp insights on rural banking, cross-border KYC, and RBI tech initiatives that makes this interview unforgettable. A powerful read for anyone needing to defend their journey while proving they're ready to lead.

Candidate Profile - Micheal MJ Hnehpuia, (Officer Branch Incharge, Scale I)

Micheal MJ Hnehpuia, a Scale 1 Officer and current Branch Incharge at Tlangnuam Branch of Mizoram Rural Bank, brings seven years of experience rooted in grassroots banking. Hailing from Lengpui, Mizoram, he began his journey as a clerk and quickly rose through the ranks due to his operational acumen and dedication. With certifications in Treasury and Credit from IIBF, along with JAIIB and CAIIB, Micheal leads full-spectrum branch operations, focusing on agricultural finance, KCC loans, and rural enterprise funding.

He has significantly improved financial literacy and credit accessibility in remote villages while boosting loan recovery rates through proactive borrower engagement. Known for his disciplined approach, Micheal is also a strong advocate of digital banking in underserved communities.

However, his journey includes personal challenges—twice suspended during his cashier tenure due to cash discrepancies. These setbacks became pivotal learning moments, transforming him into a meticulous banker. Additionally, his blunt communication and temper have occasionally strained customer relations, a weakness he is actively addressing through self-improvement and conflict resolution training

• • •

Interviewer:[*Scoffs, flipping through the file*] "So, Micheal, you expect us to promote someone who was suspended twice? Tell me, why should we trust you with a Scale 2 role when you couldn't even safeguard cash properly as a Scale 1 officer? And don't give me a rehearsed, diplomatic answer—I need the truth. Why didn't you learn your lesson after the first suspension?"

Micheal: [*Takes a deep breath, maintains a calm demeanor*] "Ma'am, I completely understand your concern. The suspensions were a hard lesson for me, and I accept full responsibility. The first suspension happened due to an unintentional error in cash balancing while handling bulk deposits. I took it as a wake-up call, but the second incident happened when I was covering for an absent colleague and rushed a transaction without double-checking. It was never about negligence, but about pressure and operational gaps that I had not yet mastered at that stage.

Since then, I have completely transformed my work ethic—I am meticulous about cash handling, I double-verify transactions, and I have trained my staff to ensure no such lapses occur again. I also implemented a maker-checker system in my branch, ensuring that no high-value transaction goes through unchecked. My past mistakes do not define my present abilities, but they have certainly shaped me into a far more responsible banker."

Interviewer: [*Leaning forward, unimpressed*] "That's a convenient excuse, isn't it? You keep talking about learning from your mistakes, but mistakes in banking are not small errors—they destroy careers. Frankly speaking, if I had my way, I wouldn't even let someone with two suspensions dream of a Scale 2 promotion. How do you justify your eligibility?"

Micheal: [*Still composed, nodding*] "I respect your perspective, Ma'am. Trust is earned, not demanded. My track record since those incidents speaks for itself. I have led my branch with zero operational discrepancies for the past three years. Under my leadership, we improved loan recovery rates by 15%, implemented strict adherence to KYC norms, and ensured seamless digital transactions for rural customers.

I understand that my past raises doubts, but if resilience, learning from failures, and leading successful banking initiatives despite setbacks do not justify eligibility, then what does?"

Interviewer:[*Huffs, but shifts gears*] "Fine. Let's talk about the work you've done as Branch Incharge in the last three years. Since you're stationed in Tlangnuam, Mizoram, tell me what specific initiatives you have taken that reflect the agricultural and cultural aspects of the North East?"

Micheal:[*Smiles slightly, relaxing into his expertise*] "Mizoram has a unique agricultural economy heavily dependent on jhum cultivation (shifting agriculture) and small-scale farming. The challenge we faced was that many farmers did not have structured credit access and were stuck in a cycle of informal lending.

In the last three years, I have focused on:

- Expanding Kisan Credit Card (KCC) outreach for tribal farmers, ensuring they have access to formal credit at subsidized interest rates.
- Introducing financial literacy camps in collaboration with local village councils and NGOs to educate farmers on loan repayment structures, reducing NPAs.
- Tailoring agricultural loans for local crops like ginger, broom grass, and passion fruit—crops that are unique to Mizoram's economy.
- Working with Self-Help Groups (SHGs) to finance women-led weaving and bamboo handicraft businesses, which are deeply tied to the region's cultural identity.

These efforts have directly contributed to financial inclusion and rural empowerment, and our branch has seen a 40% increase in agricultural loan disbursement without a corresponding spike in NPAs."

Interviewer: [*Nods slightly, but keeps a sharp tone*] "That's all well and good, but let's address a serious security issue. Your branch is located in Mizoram, which shares borders with Bangladesh and Myanmar. Illegal immigration is a concern in border states. What extra precautions does your branch take when opening new accounts to prevent fraudulent KYC applications from illegal immigrants?"

Micheal:[*Confidently*] "This is a high-priority issue, Ma'am, and we have taken several measures to ensure compliance with strict KYC norms:

- Biometric Aadhaar verification is mandatory for all new accounts.
- We cross-verify documents with local authorities to ensure that the provided Voter ID or Aadhaar card is genuine.

- For customers without proper documents, we involve Village Council Presidents (VCPs) and community leaders for verification, as they are best positioned to validate a person's local residency.
- We have flagging protocols for suspicious accounts and immediately report any irregularities to the District Administration.

Because of these measures, our branch has not processed a single fraudulent account opening related to illegal immigrants in the past three years."

Interviewer: *[Smirks]* "You seem to have a counter for everything, don't you? Let's see if you're as updated with recent RBI developments. The RBI has announced two new official domains for banks and financial firms to combat financial fraud. What are they, and when does registration start?"

Micheal:*[Without hesitation]* "Yes, Ma'am. The RBI has introduced two new official domains:

- ".bank.in" for Indian banks
- ".fin.in" for financial institutions

The primary objective is to reduce financial frauds and provide customers with a more secure, RBI-approved online presence. Registrations for these new domains begin in April."

Interviewer: *[Crosses arms, nods grudgingly]* "You've done your homework. But let's be clear—your past mistakes still make you a risky candidate. Even if your technical knowledge is strong, your behavioral reputation is a problem. You're known for being short-tempered and blunt. If you're promoted, you'll be handling even more people, bigger clients, and complex scenarios. How do you expect to manage that with your attitude?"

Micheal: *[Brief pause, nods humbly]* "Ma'am, I won't deny my weakness—I have been blunt and impatient at times. But I have been consciously working on this.

In the last three years, I have:

- Undergone soft skills training under an internal HR program.
- Practiced active listening techniques to improve interactions with customers and staff.
- Delegated work efficiently so that I don't get frustrated by micro-management pressures.

I have seen noticeable improvement, but I recognize that leadership requires continuous growth. If I am promoted, I will work even harder on my interpersonal skills to ensure I can manage my team and clients effectively."

Interviewer: [*Holds gaze for a few seconds, then sighs*] "You make a strong case, Micheal. But I'm not convinced yet. Let's move on to some advanced banking scenarios and see if you really have what it takes..."

Interviewer: "Alright, Micheal. Let's test your understanding of liquidity management. The RBI has been conducting Variable Rate Repo (VRR) auctions as a liquidity injection tool. What are VRR auctions, and under what circumstances does the RBI conduct them?"

Micheal: "Variable Rate Repo (VRR) is a short-term liquidity injection tool used by the RBI when the banking system faces liquidity deficits. It is conducted when the Weighted Average Call Money Rate (WACR) trends above the repo rate, signaling a liquidity crunch.

These auctions typically have a tenor of up to 13 days, with the cut-off rate generally staying a few basis points above the policy repo rate. For longer tenors beyond 14 days, the RBI rarely uses VRR, preferring other tools like Open Market Operations (OMO) for durable liquidity management."

Interviewer: "Not bad. Now tell me about Peer-to-Peer (P2P) lending platforms. What makes them an alternative to traditional banking, and how do they help both borrowers and lenders?"

Micheal: "P2P lending platforms directly connect borrowers with lenders through digital marketplaces, bypassing banks as intermediaries. This allows for faster, less bureaucratic loan processing, making it an attractive alternative for individuals and small businesses who face difficulties obtaining credit from formal banking channels.

For borrowers, P2P platforms offer quicker approvals, lower interest rates, and accessibility to credit despite limited collateral or credit history. For lenders, they provide higher returns and diversified investment opportunities by allowing them to fund multiple borrowers with varying risk profiles. However, due to the higher risk of default, RBI has placed caps on individual lending and borrowing limits to safeguard investors."

Interviewer: "With the rise of digital credit, the RBI is set to launch the Unified Lending Interface (ULI) soon. This is an ambitious project for frictionless credit, especially in rural areas. How do you see ULI transforming lending for small borrowers?"

Micheal: "Unified Lending Interface (ULI) is designed to make credit access faster, more transparent, and automated, especially for rural and small borrowers. By integrating financial records, bank transactions, and GST data, it allows for instant creditworthiness assessment, reducing reliance on traditional collateral-backed lending.

For rural borrowers, this means quicker loan approvals and better access to formal credit. Lenders, in turn, will benefit from AI-driven risk evaluations and a streamlined lending process. With ULI, credit disbursals that previously took weeks can now happen in minutes, making a significant impact on financial inclusion in remote areas."

Interviewer: "Let's talk about financial inclusion. Banks still struggle to penetrate rural areas efficiently. What are some of the biggest challenges banks face in financial inclusion, and how can these challenges be tackled?"

Micheal: "One major challenge is the unviability of rural branches due to high operational costs and fragmented populations, which limit banking demand. The current Business Correspondent (BC) model is restrictive, with inadequate cash delivery points, making accessibility an issue.

Another issue is low digital literacy, preventing many rural customers from fully utilizing banking services. In urban areas, slum dwellers and migrant workers struggle with KYC verification due to their frequent relocations. To address these, banks need to expand BC networks, integrate digital financial literacy programs, and adopt AI-based KYC solutions for seamless verification."

Interviewer: "Looks like you've come prepared, Micheal. One last question before we wrap this up. If I promote you to Scale 2 today, how will you handle bigger responsibilities while ensuring your past weaknesses—impatience and blunt communication—don't get in the way?"

Micheal: "I acknowledge that patience and communication have been my biggest areas of improvement. Over the past few years, I have worked on actively listening, handling conflicts diplomatically, and managing my stress levels.

To ensure this doesn't become a barrier in my leadership, I will delegate tasks more efficiently, seek mentorship from senior officers, and continue soft skills training. I believe that a good leader learns from mistakes, adapts, and continuously evolves, and I am committed to doing exactly that."

Interviewer: *[Pauses for a few seconds, then exhales deeply]* "Well, Micheal, I have to admit... you handled the grilling better than I expected. (Leans forward) You've convinced me that you've grown.

Let's see how your final evaluation turns out. That'll be all for today."

Micheal: [*Politely, with a slight smile*] "Thank you, Ma'am. I appreciate the opportunity to present myself, and I look forward to contributing more in the future."

• • •

CHAPTER IV

Disciplinary Actions, Ethical Dilemmas, and Handling Influential MLAs: Mallikarjuna Hoysala's Test of Resilience

Interview Snapshot - (Scale III to IV)

Can a senior banker bounce back from disciplinary action and still lead with integrity? This intense mock interview explores real-life dilemmas—from political pressure and cyber fraud to locker disputes and WhatsApp reporting. Mallikarjuna's responses reflect accountability, ethical strength, and sharp technical acumen in areas like trade finance, provisioning norms, and digital verification. The layered scenarios and grounded solutions make this a compelling read that sharpens judgment, builds crisis-handling instincts, and prepares you to lead with resilience and clarity in higher roles.

Candidate Profile: Mallikarjuna Hoysala (Senior Branch Manager, Scale III)

Mallikarjuna Hoysala is a seasoned banker with 15 years of extensive experience in the Indian banking sector. Currently serving as a Scale III Senior Branch Manager in Mysuru, he has demonstrated a consistent track record of leadership in branch operations, credit management, and business development. Known for his ability to navigate the complexities of rural and semi-urban banking environments, Mallikarjuna has been instrumental in driving branch profitability and customer satisfaction.

Despite facing a disciplinary action recently, which resulted in a two-increment penalty, Mallikarjuna has shown resilience by embracing the experience as an opportunity for growth. He has since strengthened his focus on risk management and compliance, turning challenges into stepping stones for improvement.

His expertise in managing teams, resolving customer grievances, and ensuring regulatory compliance makes him a well-rounded candidate for higher responsibilities, reflecting his dedication to ethical banking and continuous learning.

• • •

Interviewer: "Good morning, Mr. Mallikarjuna Hoysala. First off, congratulations on being shortlisted for this significant promotion. How are you feeling about the interview process?"

Mallikarjuna: "Good morning, Sir. Thank you so much. I feel prepared and confident but equally mindful of the importance of this moment in my career."

Interviewer: "That's great to hear, Mallikarjuna. Your career spans 15 years, including your current role as a Senior Branch Manager in Mysuru. That's a significant journey. But before we delve deeper into professional matters, let me ask you something personal. Managing work-life balance can be a challenge in this field. How do you ensure you maintain equilibrium in your personal and professional life?"

Mallikarjuna: "That's an interesting question, Sir. Over the years, I've learned the importance of time management and delegation. I ensure my weekends are reserved for family and personal growth unless there is an emergency at work. This balance keeps me motivated and effective."

Interviewer: "Excellent. Now, Mallikarjuna, I see that you recently faced disciplinary action where two of your increments were withheld. That's not a light penalty. Can you tell me what led to this situation, and more importantly, what lessons you've drawn from it?"

Mallikarjuna: "Yes, Sir, I take full responsibility for the situation. It involved lapses in monitoring a few high-value advances that turned into NPAs under my supervision. The investigation revealed that while there was no malintent, I didn't act promptly enough when early warning signals appeared. The lesson has been profound—I've become meticulous with risk monitoring and compliance. My experience has now turned into a strength as I proactively address issues before they escalate."

Interviewer: "It takes courage to own up and grow from setbacks, Mallikarjuna. Now let's pivot to a hypothetical but plausible scenario. Suppose after your promotion, you are posted as a Zonal Manager in a zone with underperforming rural branches. What strategies would you employ to help these branches achieve their business targets?"

Mallikarjuna: "Sir, rural branches often face unique challenges like limited customer base or dependency on seasonal income. My approach would involve:

- Conducting branch-wise analysis to identify specific issues, like credit portfolio quality or lack of staff motivation.

- Organizing training sessions for branch staff to improve customer service and cross-selling skills.
- Encouraging participation in government schemes like PMEGP or SHG financing, which can drive both social impact and business.
- Partnering with local influencers or farmer groups to increase financial literacy.
- Lastly, encouraging healthy competition among branches by offering small incentives for achieving targets."

Interviewer: "That's quite a structured approach. Let me throw you a curveball now. Many zonal or regional offices these days require daily reporting on WhatsApp groups. Do you think using such platforms for professional reporting is appropriate? Why or why not?"

Mallikarjuna: "Sir, while WhatsApp is convenient and widely used, it is not an ideal platform for official communication. Key concerns include:

- Data privacy and security risks, especially with sensitive customer and business information.
- Lack of formal documentation, which could create accountability issues.
- Increased stress among staff due to round-the-clock messages.

Instead, I'd recommend using secure internal platforms like intranet portals or official emails for reporting."

Interviewer: "Fair point. Speaking of dilemmas, let's address a challenging ethical scenario. Suppose a senior colleague verbally instructs you over the phone to manipulate certain records for personal gain. How would you handle this?"

Mallikarjuna: "Sir, ethical integrity is non-negotiable for me. Here's how I would respond:

- Politely but firmly decline the instruction, citing regulatory and policy constraints.
- Document the conversation immediately, noting the time, date, and content of the call.
- If the pressure persists, I would escalate the issue to the appropriate authority, like the vigilance department or my reporting officer.
- Make sure all actions are taken voluntarily and thoughtfully, while safeguarding my legal and professional interests. Handling such

situations calmly but decisively is critical."

Interviewer: "That's a textbook answer, Mallikarjuna. Now, coming back to something more technical. Can you explain the difference between fund-based and non-fund-based credit facilities? And why is the latter gaining traction these days?"

Mallikarjuna: "Certainly, Sir. Fund-based facilities, like term loans and cash credit, involve direct disbursement of funds to the borrower. Non-fund-based facilities, like guarantees and letters of credit, create contingent liabilities without immediate fund outflow.
Non-fund-based products are gaining popularity due to their lower capital requirements for banks and reduced interest burden for customers."

Interviewer: "Spot on. Another technical question—what are the key differences between provisioning norms for standard assets and NPAs? How do they impact profitability?"

Mallikarjuna: "Sir, provisioning for standard assets is a precautionary measure and is much lower, typically around 0.40%-1%, depending on the sector. For NPAs, provisioning depends on the asset classification—sub-standard, doubtful, or loss—and can range from 15% to 100%.
Higher provisioning for NPAs directly impacts profitability by reducing net earnings, making asset quality a critical focus area."

Interviewer: "Impressive, Mallikarjuna. Let's shift gears slightly. With the advent of AI in banking, how do you see the role of branch managers evolving?"

Mallikarjuna: "AI will automate routine tasks like KYC, loan processing, and data analytics, allowing branch managers to focus more on customer relationships, business development, and strategic decision-making. However, continuous upskilling will be essential to adapt to these changes."

Interviewer: "One easy question before we proceed further. Do you think regional rural banks (RRBs) should be merged with their sponsor banks for better efficiency?"

Mallikarjuna: "It's a debatable topic, Sir. While mergers could bring in better technology and managerial expertise, RRBs cater to niche rural markets with specific needs. Any decision should balance efficiency with the inclusivity goals for rural banking."

Interviewer: "Alright Mallikarjuna, let's delve into some more scenarios to test your practical judgment and technical expertise. These are the kinds of challenges you might face in your new role, should you be promoted.

Let's begin."

Interviewer: "Suppose the MLA of your region visits your branch and tries to influence you into sanctioning loans for certain individuals. While maintaining cordial relations with the MLA, how would you handle such a situation?"

Mallikarjuna: "Sir, this is a delicate situation that requires balancing professional ethics with maintaining good relations. Here's how I would handle it:

- I would respectfully explain that all loans are sanctioned based on merit and adherence to bank policies.
- To keep the MLA's trust, I would offer to prioritize the processing of applications if they meet our guidelines.
- Additionally, I would emphasize the importance of compliance with banking regulations, which safeguard both the customer and the bank.
- If the pressure becomes excessive, I'd escalate the matter to my reporting authority while keeping it diplomatic."

Interviewer: "Well balanced. Now let's consider a different type of crisis. Suppose a locker in your branch was forcibly broken into, and the customer is demanding a compensation of ₹5 crores, claiming valuables worth that amount were stolen. How would you manage this situation?"

Mallikarjuna: "Sir, locker agreements clearly state that the bank's liability is limited to maintaining the physical security of the lockers, not the contents. Here's how I would address the situation:

- Immediately inform the customer about the terms of the locker agreement.
- Conduct a thorough investigation of the incident, involving law enforcement if needed.
- Offer assistance to the customer in filing a police report or claiming insurance, if they have coverage.
- If the customer persists, I would escalate the matter to the legal team and provide them with all relevant details."

Interviewer: "Sound approach, Mallikarjuna. Let's switch to something more technical now. Digital verification is becoming critical. How would you verify the various documents submitted by a corporate borrower digitally?"

Mallikarjuna: "Digital verification can streamline processes significantly. Here's what I would do:

- Verify the PAN and GSTIN through government portals to confirm the borrower's legal identity.
- Check financial statements and filings on the Ministry of Corporate Affairs (MCA) portal.
- Use third-party platforms like CIBIL or Experian for credit history verification.
- Authenticate ownership and encumbrance status of collateral through land records or asset registries.
- For further scrutiny, rely on digital forensics tools and request audited documents for cross-verification."

Interviewer: "Good grasp on this. Now let's discuss trade finance. Can you explain the difference between an inland letter of credit and a foreign letter of credit?"

Mallikarjuna: "Certainly, Sir. An inland letter of credit is used for domestic trade within the country, while a foreign letter of credit facilitates international trade.

- Inland LCs are governed primarily by domestic laws, whereas foreign LCs are governed by international regulations such as UCP 600.
- Inland LCs deal with Indian rupees, while foreign LCs usually involve foreign currencies.
- Foreign LCs often require compliance with additional trade agreements or customs regulations."

Interviewer: "Well put. Now, one final question before we conclude. With the rise in cyber fraud, how would you ensure robust security measures are in place at your branch?"

Mallikarjuna: "Cybersecurity is a top priority, Sir. I would:

- Ensure all systems are equipped with updated antivirus and firewall protections.
- Conduct regular training for staff to recognize phishing attempts and other scams.

- Implement multi-factor authentication for all critical systems and customer accounts.
- Regularly audit the IT systems and follow RBI's guidelines on cybersecurity.
- Set up a quick-response protocol for reporting and managing incidents promptly."

Interviewer: "Mallikarjuna, you've shown a strong grasp of technical knowledge, leadership, and ethical decision-making throughout this interview. This kind of well-rounded understanding is exactly what's needed for higher responsibilities. Thank you for your time, and I wish you the best for the next stages of this process."

Mallikarjuna: "Thank you so much, Sir. It's been an enriching experience, and I'm grateful for the opportunity."

• • •

CHAPTER V

From Comfort Zone to Crisis Zones: How Judhajit Roy Tackles Banking's Toughest Challenges in his Interview

Interview Snapshot - (Scale II to III)

What does it take to move from a comfort zone to a commanding role in banking? This mock interview with Judhajit Roy offers a masterclass in handling real-world credit cases, HR dilemmas, NPAs, and green financing. His thoughtful responses, practical scenarios, and technical clarity make this a must-read for anyone preparing for a Scale 2 or Scale 3 interview. If you're aiming to level up in your banking career, this interview reveals the mindset and preparation needed to stand out.

Candidate Profile: Judhajit Roy (Credit Manager, Scale II)

Judhajit Roy is a dedicated banking professional currently serving as a Scale 2 Officer in the capacity of Credit Manager in Kolkata. With over a decade of experience in retail credit, Judhajit has developed expertise in managing and processing diverse loan portfolios, including housing loans, education loans, and personal loans. His in-depth understanding of credit assessment, risk management, and customer service has been instrumental in maintaining the quality of the bank's credit portfolio.

Throughout his career, Judhajit has consistently demonstrated his ability to navigate complex financial scenarios and deliver tailored solutions for clients, reflecting his strong analytical skills and commitment to excellence. Notably, Judhajit's entire banking journey has been rooted in Kolkata, where he has gained profound insights into the city's financial dynamics. His focus on professional growth and his proactive approach make him a strong contender for higher responsibilities within the banking sector.

• • •

Interviewer: "Good morning, Mr. Roy, and congratulations on being shortlisted for the promotion interview!"

Judhajit: "Good morning, Sir, and thank you very much. It's an honor to be here."

Interviewer: "Judhajit, I see you've been with the bank for over a decade now and are currently a Credit Manager in Kolkata. You must have handled a variety of credit proposals. What has been your toughest proposal to date, and how did you manage it?"

Judhajit: "Sir, one of the toughest proposals I handled was a housing project financing request from a mid-sized builder during the pandemic. The builder's financials showed irregularities, and while the project had potential, it required meticulous risk assessment. I worked extensively with the legal and technical teams to address land title issues, ensured compliance with RERA, and structured the loan to mitigate risks. Eventually, the proposal was approved with conditions, and the project succeeded, strengthening both the builder's and the bank's credibility."

Interviewer: "That must have been a challenging yet rewarding experience. Since you've worked extensively with housing projects, what precautions do you take while handling proposals from builders, especially for housing societies?"

Judhajit: "Sir, while dealing with builder proposals, I prioritize verifying the land titles and project approvals to avoid legal disputes. I ensure the builder's past projects have been completed satisfactorily and on time. Compliance with RERA is non-negotiable. I also look for builder-buyer agreements that are transparent and fair. Lastly, cash flow analysis is critical to ensure the builder has adequate funds for project completion."

Interviewer: "You've clearly refined your skills and knowledge. Now let's consider a hypothetical scenario. Suppose you're posted in a coastal city, and you find it tough to meet the bank's advance targets. What would you do?"

Judhajit: "Sir, in such a situation, I would adopt a multi-pronged strategy. Firstly, I'd focus on understanding the local economic drivers—such as fisheries, tourism, and maritime industries—and design tailor-made loan products. Collaborating with local chambers of commerce to conduct financial literacy camps can help generate leads. Secondly, I'd leverage existing clients for cross-selling opportunities and referrals. Lastly, I'd ensure high service standards to build trust and attract more customers."

Interviewer: "Creative thinking is essential in such roles. Judhajit, I understand your wife is also in the same bank. If both of you are posted to different locations, how would you handle this professionally and personally?"

(In an interview, it's important to approach this question diplomatically. While

it's common in reality to seek home or same-location postings after promotion, your response should focus on highlighting your adaptability and professional commitment—similar to the reply shared below.)

Judhajit: "Sir, while it may be challenging, we are prepared for such situations. Professionally, we would prioritize our respective roles, ensuring no compromises on our responsibilities. Personally, we'd plan our leaves strategically and stay connected through regular communication. We are committed to managing any situation that arises."

Interviewer: "It's commendable that you have a clear plan for such scenarios. Now, let's switch gears. Do you think the subsidies given by the government to farmers are beneficial in the long run?"

Judhajit: "Sir, subsidies are essential in supporting farmers, especially during crises. However, they should be complemented by initiatives that improve productivity and reduce dependency on subsidies—like investments in irrigation, technology, and market linkages. Over-reliance on subsidies can strain government resources and may discourage self-reliance."

Interviewer: "An insightful perspective. Let's delve into another hypothetical. Suppose you're posted in the Coimbatore Zone's Controlling Office as an Administration Manager. You notice two lady clerks at a branch are consistently late, and this is affecting branch operations. What steps would you take?"

Judhajit: "Sir, I'd address this situation tactfully. First, I'd verify the biometric attendance records to confirm the pattern. Then, I'd have a private conversation with the clerks to understand their reasons. If it's a genuine issue, I'd explore solutions like flexible timings. If not, I'd counsel them on the importance of punctuality. If tardiness persists, I'd escalate it per the bank's disciplinary policies."

Interviewer: "Well said. Let me ask a technical question now. How do you assess a borrower's repayment capacity while processing a loan?"

Judhajit: "Sir, I evaluate the borrower's income sources, stability, and monthly obligations to calculate the Debt-to-Income ratio. Additionally, I analyze their credit history and repayment track record, check for sufficient collateral or guarantees, and factor in industry risks or economic conditions."

Interviewer: "Good. Can you tell me how the MCLR system works?"

Judhajit: "Certainly, Sir. The Marginal Cost of Funds-based Lending Rate is a benchmark for setting loan interest rates. It considers factors like the marginal cost of funds, operating costs, negative carry on CRR, and tenor premium. This ensures transparency and links loan rates closely to the cost of funds."

Interviewer: "Excellent. Let's move to another pressing topic. What are your views on rising NPAs in retail loans, and how can they be controlled?"

Judhajit: "Sir, the rise in retail NPAs is concerning, driven by factors like over-leveraging and economic instability. To control this, banks must strengthen due diligence processes, use predictive analytics to identify stressed accounts, and promote financial literacy to help borrowers manage debt better."

Interviewer: "Judhajit, you've stayed in Kolkata throughout your career. Do you think working outside your comfort zone could enhance your professional growth?"

Judhajit: "Absolutely, Sir. Working in different regions would expose me to diverse customer profiles, economic conditions, and operational challenges. This would enhance my adaptability, problem-solving skills, and understanding of the bank's functioning at a broader level."

Interviewer: "A valid point. One final question for now—what is your understanding of green financing, and how can banks contribute to environmental sustainability?"

Judhajit: "Sir, green financing involves funding projects that promote environmental sustainability, like renewable energy and waste management. Banks can contribute by offering concessional rates for green initiatives, issuing green bonds, and encouraging eco-friendly business practices among borrowers."

Interviewer: "Thank you, Mr. Roy. Your responses reflect a strong understanding of banking operations and demonstrate your readiness for higher responsibilities. I appreciate the clarity and depth of your answers."

Judhajit: "Thank you very much, Sir. It has been a great experience to discuss these topics with you, and I look forward to contributing even more to the bank in a leadership role."

Interviewer: "We wish you all the best for your promotion. Keep this level of confidence and knowledge with you, and I am sure you'll excel in any role assigned to you."

Judhajit: "Thank you, Sir. I am truly grateful for this opportunity and will continue to strive for excellence."

Interviewer: "That's the spirit! You may leave now. Have a good day."
Judhajit: "Good day, Sir."

• • •

CHAPTER VI

From Munnar to Punjab: How B Renuka Plans to Break Language Barriers and Lead a Rural Branch

Interview Snapshot - (Scale I to II)
What happens when a banker from Kerala is suddenly tasked with leading a rural branch in Punjab? This gripping mock interview takes you through real-world challenges like language barriers, flood evacuation, suspicious transactions, overdue KCC loans, and digital transformation. Renuka's sharp responses reflect resilience, leadership, and a customer-first mindset. Her ability to blend regulatory knowledge with emotional intelligence makes this interview a compelling read packed with lessons, strategies, and insights every banking aspirant needs to know before facing the panel.

Candidate Profile - B Renuka (Assistant Manager, Scale I)
B Renuka, currently serving as an Officer Scale 1 in Munnar, Kerala, brings three years of hands-on experience in managing general banking operations. Her academic credentials, including an MBA in Finance, coupled with her Credit Professional certification, underscore her deep understanding of banking principles and credit risk management. Renuka's tenure in a picturesque yet demanding branch environment has honed her adaptability, customer relationship skills, and operational expertise. She has consistently demonstrated a proactive approach to problem-solving and a commitment to professional growth, evident in her pursuit of advanced certifications. With her solid foundation in banking and finance, Renuka is well-poised to take on leadership responsibilities in a higher role.

• • •

Interviewer: "Good morning, Ms. Renuka, and congratulations on clearing the Scale 2 written examination."

Renuka: "Good morning, Sir. Thank you very much. It's an honor to be here."

Interviewer: "You've been working as an Officer Scale 1 in Munnar for the last three years, right? A beautiful location indeed. How has your journey been so far?"

Renuka: "Yes, Sir, Munnar is breathtaking. My journey has been enriching. Handling general banking operations has taught me not only technical skills but also how to connect with customers from diverse backgrounds."

Interviewer: "That's great to hear. Now, just imagine after your promotion, you're being transferred from the serene hills of Kerala to take charge of a rural branch in Punjab. Let's talk about the obvious challenge: the language. You don't speak Punjabi, right? So, how would you manage the language barrier in such a scenario?"

Renuka: "No, Sir. While I don't speak Punjabi, I believe communication is about understanding and intent. I'd rely on bilingual staff, build rapport with influential locals like Sarpanches, and even use tools like translation apps for immediate needs. Additionally, I'd start learning Punjabi to bridge the gap."

Interviewer:*[smiling]* "A proactive approach. But what about legal documents like land papers, often written in Punjabi? How would you ensure accurate processing of such papers?"

Renuka: "Sir, I'd engage experienced staff or advocates familiar with the local language to assist in scrutinizing documents. Additionally, I'd request a notarized English translation for critical cases. My focus would be on ensuring compliance while minimizing errors."

Interviewer: "That's a practical solution. Let's dive into another real-world scenario. Imagine a new clerk joins your branch in Punjab. What would be the first instructions you give them on their day of joining?"

Renuka: "Sir, I'd emphasize the importance of adhering to operational guidelines and being vigilant in cash handling. I'd explain their role in building customer trust and maintaining branch decorum. Lastly, I'd familiarize them with the customer service ethos and fraud prevention measures."

Interviewer: "Good start. Let's add a twist. You're now the branch manager, and Punjab's infamous overseas migration issue comes to your desk. How would you transform this challenge into a business opportunity for your branch?"

Renuka: "Sir, I'd position the branch as a hub for remittance services, targeting NRIs and their families. I'd also market investment products like NRI fixed deposits and help them leverage home loans for property investments in India. Collaborating with financial advisors for overseas clients could further boost our visibility and revenue."

Interviewer:[*leaning forward*] "Interesting perspective. Speaking of certifications, tell me how you'd explain the importance of Credit Professional certification to your team."

Renuka: "Sir, I'd highlight how this certification equips us to assess creditworthiness, minimize NPAs, and structure loans efficiently. It's not just about learning concepts but applying them to ensure the bank's profitability and customer satisfaction."

Interviewer: "Excellent. Now, let's test your problem-solving skills. Suppose your branch is located near a river that is flooding due to heavy rains. The government authorities have issued evacuation orders for the area. You have panicked customers in the branch demanding assistance with cash withdrawals and other urgent needs. How will you manage this situation while ensuring the safety of your staff and customers?"

Renuka: "Sir, in such a critical situation, safety would be my foremost priority. I'd immediately coordinate with local authorities to understand evacuation protocols and timelines. Simultaneously, I'd address customers' concerns by organizing a quick and orderly process for cash withdrawals, ensuring that high-priority needs are met within the time available.

I'd also notify nearby branches that are operational and unaffected, guiding customers to those locations for uninterrupted service. To safeguard documents and assets, I'd ensure the branch's cash and records are secured and, if possible, moved to a safer location. Staff safety would be paramount, so I'd ensure they are evacuated promptly once critical tasks are completed. Clear communication and maintaining calm would be key to handling such a situation efficiently."

Interviewer: "Good contingency planning. Let's add another layer of complexity. Your rural branch reports a sudden surge in overdue KCC loans due to crop failure. Farmers are distressed. How will you handle recovery while maintaining goodwill?"

Renuka: "Sir, recovery in such cases needs empathy and strategy. I'd initiate discussions with farmer groups, exploring restructuring options like moratoriums or extending tenures. Government schemes or subsidies could provide relief. Building trust is critical to balancing recovery with relationship management."

Interviewer: "Impressive approach. Now let's move to a broader topic. How do you think India's digital banking revolution has impacted rural banking, and how can you leverage it in your branch?"

Renuka: "Sir, digital banking has democratized financial services, even in rural areas. I'd promote digital literacy, onboarding customers to use UPI, mobile banking, and digital wallets. Campaigns demonstrating the safety and convenience of these tools would drive adoption and reduce branch workload."

Interviewer: "A necessary push toward modernization. One last question before we start winding up. With interest rate fluctuations becoming a concern, how would you guide your branch to handle loan repricing and maintain profitability?"

Renuka: "Sir, I'd ensure timely repricing of loans aligned with MCLR or external benchmarks, safeguarding the bank's margins. Simultaneously, diversifying the branch's portfolio by promoting fixed-rate products could mitigate risks from volatile rates."

Interviewer: "Before we conclude, let's put you in another hypothetical situation. Imagine a customer visits your branch in Punjab and deposits a large sum of   ₹30 lakhs in cash. You notice discrepancies in his documentation, and his responses raise suspicions. How would you handle this situation?"

Renuka: "Sir, I'd remain polite but vigilant. First, I'd ensure adherence to the KYC norms by verifying all documentation thoroughly. If the discrepancies persist, I'd escalate the matter to our compliance department, filing a Suspicious Transaction Report (STR) as per RBI guidelines. Ensuring proper documentation and reporting would safeguard the bank's interests and ensure regulatory compliance."

Interviewer: *[raising an eyebrow]* "Good answer. Let's shift to another important topic. You're aware of the financial inclusion efforts in rural areas. As a branch manager, how would you boost financial literacy and inclusion in your rural branch?"

Renuka: "Sir, financial inclusion requires a multi-faceted approach. I'd organize regular financial literacy camps in collaboration with local bodies, emphasizing the importance of savings, insurance, and credit. Additionally, I'd introduce no-frills accounts, PMJDY schemes, and microloans tailored to the community's needs. Leveraging SHGs and MFIs could also enhance outreach and impact."

Interviewer: "A comprehensive strategy. Finally, here's a personal question. Your current role in Munnar has given you an edge in handling customers and operations. How has this experience shaped you as a banker, and how will it influence your future roles?"

Renuka: "Sir, working in Munnar has been transformative. I've gained a deep understanding of customer-centric banking, enhanced my ability to multitask effectively under pressure, and developed the skills to navigate a wide range of challenges with confidence.These experiences have instilled confidence and resilience, qualities I'll carry forward to lead teams effectively and contribute to the bank's growth in my future roles."

Interviewer: *[nodding thoughtfully]* "That's an insightful perspective, Renuka. You've demonstrated a good balance of technical knowledge, practical application, and leadership potential. It was a pleasure interacting with you, and I wish you the very best for your promotion."

Renuka: "Thank you so much, Sir. I truly appreciate this opportunity and your valuable insights."

• • •

CHAPTER VII

From a Militancy-Hit Village to a Bank Officer? The Inspiring & Unfiltered Promotion Interview of Irfan Ahmad Dar

Interview Snapshot - (Clerical to Scale I)

This interview is a rare blend of inspiration and realism. It captures how a frontline clerk from a conflict zone transforms hardship into purpose, while confidently tackling tough questions on repo rates, reverse mortgages, credit utilization, and lien limitations. Irfan's honest learning moment, his prioritization during a branch crisis, and his empathetic approach to digital resistance reveal exactly what interviewers look for in future officers. A must-read for those looking to stand out through authenticity, technical clarity, and grounded leadership.

Candidate Profile: Irfan Ahmad Dar(Clerk)

Irfan Ahmad Dar, currently working as a Clerk in Srinagar, Jammu & Kashmir, exemplifies resilience, service, and ambition. With six years of experience in front-line banking operations, he handles account opening, KYC compliance, cashier duties, passbook updates, and cheque clearing with precision and integrity. Certified in JAIIB, Digital Banking, and Customer Relationship Management, Irfan plays a key role in ensuring smooth customer service while promoting financial literacy and digital inclusion in his rural community.

Hailing from a militancy-affected village in Anantnag district, Irfan's journey is marked by courage and determination. As the first public sector bank employee from his village, he shoulders the dual responsibility of supporting his family and serving as a role model for the youth around him. His greatest personal challenge lies in managing financial and emotional responsibilities for his younger siblings while navigating the daily complexities of life in a conflict zone.

Despite limited exposure to credit and lending, Irfan is committed to learning and growing. He is currently preparing for the CAIIB exam and aspires to become a Scale 1 Officer—the first from his village. His unwavering dedication to community upliftment and professional excellence positions him as a strong candidate for advancement in the banking sector.

• • •

Interviewer: "Good morning, Mr. Irfan. I've gone through your profile, and I must say, your journey is truly inspiring. You come from a remote village in Anantnag, and now you are here, preparing for your promotion. That's no small feat! Tell me, how did you find your way into banking from a place that has faced decades of turmoil?"

Irfan Ahmad Dar: "Good morning, sir! It has been a journey filled with challenges and resilience. Coming from a militancy-affected village, opportunities were scarce, but my father always believed in the power of education. I worked hard, pursued my graduation while managing financial difficulties, and cracked the bank exam despite the odds. My selection was a turning point—not just for me but for my entire village. People who once saw government jobs as distant dreams now ask me how they can prepare for banking and other competitive exams. This job is not just my career; it's my way of bringing hope to my community."

Interviewer: "That's incredible, Irfan. Your determination is commendable. Now, given your background, you've seen firsthand how instability affects education. Why do you think education is particularly important in militancy-hit regions like yours?"

Irfan Ahmad Dar: "Sir, education is the strongest weapon against ignorance and extremism. In places like mine, where fear and misinformation often dictate choices, education brings awareness, employment, and financial independence. It provides youth with alternatives—an opportunity to build careers rather than being drawn into destructive paths. The more educated our youth become, the fewer will fall prey to radical ideologies. I want to see a day when children in my village dream of being bankers, doctors, and engineers rather than feeling trapped by circumstances."

Interviewer: "Well said! That vision is exactly what the country needs. Now, shifting gears to banking, let's test your technical knowledge. Can you explain what Performance Guarantees are?"

Irfan Ahmad Dar: "Yes, sir. Performance Guarantees are financial instruments issued by banks on behalf of customers to guarantee their performance as per the contracts they enter into. The bank doesn't take on the obligations of the contract itself but commits to making financial payments in case the customer defaults. If the customer fails to fulfill their contractual obligations, the bank makes the payment under the guarantee upon notification of default."

Interviewer: "Spot on! Now, let's discuss a recent banking development. The RBI has recently cut the repo rate by 25 basis points to 6.25%—the first such cut in five years. What impact will this have on our economy?"

Irfan Ahmad Dar: "Sir, I believe a reduction in repo rate means banks will have to pay a higher interest rate to RBI, which might lead to an increase in lending rates for customers."

Interviewer: "Hold on, Irfan. That's not quite right. It's actually the opposite. A repo rate cut makes borrowing cheaper for banks, which means they can reduce lending rates for customers. This encourages businesses and individuals to take loans, thereby boosting consumption and investment. Lower interest rates often lead to higher economic growth. However, if not managed properly, excessive borrowing can lead to inflationary pressures."

Irfan Ahmad Dar: "Understood, sir. Thank you for correcting me. This helps me understand the concept better."

Interviewer: "That's the spirit! Learning never stops in banking. Moving to another important product—Reverse Mortgage Loan. What is it, and how does it work?"

Irfan Ahmad Dar: "Reverse Mortgage Loan (RML) is a scheme designed for senior citizens above 60 years. It allows them to receive periodic payments from the bank against the mortgage of their house, while they continue to live in and own the property. The key feature is that they do not have to repay the loan during their lifetime. Under Section 10(43) of the Income Tax Act, these payments are also exempt from income tax. If the borrower outlives the loan tenure, they can still remain in the house as long as it is used as their primary residence."

Interviewer: "Correct! This product is particularly beneficial for retired individuals who need financial support but do not want to sell their homes. Now, let's add a practical twist. Suppose you are the Branch Manager, and an elderly couple approaches you for a Reverse Mortgage Loan. However, their property has a legal dispute regarding ownership. How would you handle this situation?"

Irfan Ahmad Dar: "Sir, in such a case, I would first verify the nature of the dispute through legal records. Since banks can only mortgage legally clear properties, I would advise the couple to resolve the ownership issue before applying for the loan. Meanwhile, I would guide them on other possible options, such as availing government pensions or fixed deposits, to manage their finances temporarily."

Interviewer: "Smart response! Practical problem-solving is key for an officer. Now, let's test your ability to handle pressure. Imagine this—you are the only officer present in the branch due to staff shortages. A customer urgently needs a Demand Draft (DD) for a medical emergency, a cash deposit queue is piling up, and at the same time, a major clearing transaction needs verification. How will you prioritize?"

Irfan Ahmad Dar: "In such a scenario, I would remain calm and prioritize based on urgency and time sensitivity. The medical emergency requires immediate action, so I would issue the DD first. Next, I would briefly inform customers in the deposit queue about the situation and process their transactions as efficiently as possible. Lastly, since clearing transactions have a designated cut-off time, I would ensure it is completed before the deadline. Additionally, I would try to involve available clerical staff to manage the queue while I handle verification."

Interviewer: "Excellent prioritization! This is the kind of decision-making expected from a Scale-1 officer. Now, let's bring in a customer service scenario. An elderly woman comes in, confused about digital banking. She fears online fraud and refuses to use UPI, insisting on withdrawing cash every time. How would you convince her to adopt digital banking?"

Irfan Ahmad Dar: "Sir, I would first empathize with her concerns and explain digital banking in simple terms. I would assure her of the safety measures banks have in place—such as two-factor authentication and SMS alerts. To build trust, I would guide her through a small, controlled UPI transaction, like recharging her phone. If she remains hesitant, I would introduce her to services like SMS banking and net banking with limited transactions. My aim would be to make her comfortable rather than forcing adoption."

Interviewer: "That's the right approach—educating rather than pushing. Now, before we proceed further, tell me, Irfan, why do you believe you deserve this promotion to officer grade?"

Irfan Ahmad Dar: "Sir, I have given six years of dedicated service in banking operations, ensuring compliance, customer satisfaction, and digital awareness in my region. My experience as a teller, clearing clerk, and account opening officer has strengthened my understanding of branch functioning.This promotion isn't just a career step for me; it's a statement that perseverance and education can overcome any barrier. I am ready to take on higher responsibilities and contribute to financial inclusion at a larger scale."

Interviewer: "Irfan, before we conclude, I have a few more questions covering important banking concepts. Let's start with this—CIBIL Score is a three-digit numeric summary of a customer's credit history. What is the range of a CIBIL Score?"

Irfan Ahmad Dar: "Sir, the CIBIL Score ranges from 300 to 900, where a higher score indicates better creditworthiness."

Interviewer: "That's right. A good score, typically above 750, increases the chances of loan approvals and better credit terms. Now, let's consider a customer service scenario. Mr. Jagan Reddy, an officer at a rural branch in West Bengal, receives a written complaint from a local farmer about non-credit of his interest subsidy. Since the farmer doesn't understand English, he responds in Bengali with the help of local staff. What aspect of service quality did the officer meet?"

Irfan Ahmad Dar: "Sir, this falls under the "Empathy" dimension of service quality. Specifically, he addressed three key expectations: accessibility, communication, and understanding the customer. By responding in Bengali, he ensured the customer could comprehend the reply, fostering trust and transparency."

Interviewer: "Exactly! Service quality is not just about processing transactions but also about making customers feel understood and valued. Moving forward, consider two individuals with the same sanctioned credit limit of   ₹5,00,000. Mr. A uses only   ₹50,000, while Mr. B fully utilizes ₹5,00,000 and requests an additional   ₹50,000. Whose credit score is likely to improve?"

Irfan Ahmad Dar: "Mr. A's credit score will improve, sir. Effective credit utilization plays a significant role in determining an individual's credit score. Since Mr. A is using only a small portion of his sanctioned limit, he is considered a low-risk borrower. On the other hand, Mr. B, by fully utilizing his limit and seeking more credit, might be seen as overleveraged, which could negatively impact his score."

Interviewer: "That's the correct analysis. Low credit utilization signals financial discipline, which lenders prefer. Now suppose a customer at your branch wants to authorize his brother to operate his bank account while he is abroad. He asks you what kind of legal authorization is required. How would you explain it to him?"

Irfan Ahmad Dar: "Sir, I would inform him that he needs to issue a "Mandate." A mandate is a written authority given by the account holder in favor of a third person, authorizing them to operate the account on their behalf. This is useful for individuals who may not be physically present but need someone they trust to manage their banking transactions."

Interviewer: "That's the perfect way to explain it. A Power of Attorney is another alternative, but a mandate is generally used for simpler, day-to-day operations. Now, in banking, the "Right to Lien" allows a bank to retain possession of a customer's assets in case of non-payment. But in which situations can a bank not exercise its right to lien?"

Irfan Ahmad Dar: "Sir, banks cannot exercise lien in the following cases:

- Safe custody articles.
- Documents or money deposited for a specific purpose.
- Articles left negligently in the bank premises.
- If the debt has not yet matured.
- If the goods or securities deposited with the bank have been stolen by the customer and belong to the rightful owner."

Interviewer: "Correct! Lien is a powerful right, but it comes with limitations to ensure fairness and protect customers' interests. Now, Irfan, this brings us to the final part of our interview. Tell me—if you are promoted to an officer, what changes would you bring to your branch and the banking experience for customers?"

Irfan Ahmad Dar: "Sir, my first priority as an officer would be improving customer awareness of digital banking. In rural areas like mine, many customers still hesitate to use UPI, internet banking, or even ATMs. I would conduct financial literacy camps to help them transition to safer and more convenient banking methods. Secondly, I would focus on enhancing operational efficiency—reducing turnaround time for services like account opening and cheque clearing. Finally, I would ensure better grievance redressal, making sure customers, especially the elderly, feel heard and respected. With this promotion, I want to set an example for my community and show that banking is not just about transactions—it's about transforming lives."

Interviewer: "That's an inspiring closing statement, Irfan. I must say, your commitment to banking and financial inclusion is evident. You have the technical knowledge, customer service skills, and the right mindset to be an officer. Thank you for this insightful discussion, and best of luck for your promotion interview!"

● ● ●

42

CHAPTER VIII

Cracking the Bank Promotion Code: How Jagan Mastered Complex Scenarios

Interview Snapshot - (Scale I to II)

This interview offers a rich blend of practical insights, technical accuracy, and smart scenario handling. Jagan confidently navigates questions on recovery without SARFAESI, cash disbursal during outages, AML red flags, and customer retention strategies. His responses show a balanced approach to compliance, customer service, and crisis management. With bonus touches on AI in banking, Mudra loans, and green initiatives, this is an excellent read to refine your answering style, strengthen concepts, and understand how to approach complex situations with clarity and confidence.

Candidate Profile : Jagan (Assistant Manager, Scale I)

Jagan is a committed and well-rounded banking professional with five years of experience, having joined as a Probationary Officer. Known for his adaptability and customer focused approach, he has worked extensively in rural banking, gaining hands-on experience in credit, recovery, and branch operations. A CAIIB qualifier, Jagan is currently preparing for the Certified Credit Professional Examination, reflecting his dedication to continuous learning. His ability to handle operational challenges, motivate teams, and deliver innovative solutions sets him apart.

• • •

Interviewer: "Congratulations, Mr. Jagan, on clearing the written examination for your promotion. It must feel great to have reached this stage."

    Jagan: "Thank you, sir. It is indeed a significant milestone in my career, and I'm excited about this opportunity."

    Interviewer: "I see from your profile that you joined the bank five years ago as a Probationary Officer. However, you're applying for the promotion a little late. Why is that?"

(Be prepared for this question if you are applying for promotion bit late)

Jagan: "Sir, my wife was pursuing her PhD from Vizag University, and supporting her academic journey was a priority for me. She completed her studies last year, and I felt this was the right time to focus on my professional growth."

Interviewer: "That's admirable. It's important to strike a balance between personal commitments and professional aspirations."

Jagan: "Thank you, sir."

Interviewer: "Since you're appearing for the Scale 1 to 2 promotion, there's a high probability of being posted as a Branch Manager in a rural area. Recovery in rural areas, particularly for agricultural advances, can be quite challenging since SARFAESI doesn't apply to agricultural land. How would you handle recovery in such cases?"

Jagan: "Sir, during my current tenure at a rural branch, I've had the opportunity to accompany my Branch Manager on recovery visits. We often engage with influential village leaders such as gram pradhans to mediate. Their involvement usually encourages borrowers to make repayments. While it's a tedious process, persistence and building trust within the community have yielded positive results. I would adopt a similar approach and explore other innovative methods if required."

Interviewer: "That's a sensible and pragmatic approach."

Interviewer: "You've also cleared CAIIB. Can you explain bid rates and ask rates in the banking context?"

Jagan: "Certainly, sir. Bid rates are the prices at which banks buy foreign currency, while ask rates are the prices at which banks sell foreign currency."

Interviewer: "That's correct. What are your plans after clearing CAIIB?"

Jagan: "I'm currently preparing for the Certified Credit Professional Examination to enhance my knowledge of credit management and decision-making."

Interviewer: "Continuous learning is a commendable habit. Let's move to a hypothetical scenario. Suppose your rural branch faces a connectivity issue for three consecutive days. Customers grow restless and demand their payments. How would you handle this situation if the connectivity issue persists for another three or four days?"

Jagan: "Sir, such situations demand creative problem-solving. I would send a staff member to the nearest branch with connectivity. At our branch, we'd verify withdrawal forms manually and communicate the details to the officer at the connected branch for validation. He will debit or post the entries. Once the transaction(i.e. Account is debited) is confirmed, we'd proceed with disbursing the cash locally. This ensures customer satisfaction, safety of bank staff and operational accuracy, even under challenging circumstances."

Interviewer: "That's an innovative and effective approach. Well done.Now what can you tell me about reverse mortgage loans?"

Jagan: "Reverse mortgages provide senior citizens with a source of income against the mortgage of their self-occupied property. Payments are made periodically to the borrower, allowing them financial security in their later years."

Interviewer: "Correct. Let's shift gears to anti-money laundering. Imagine a customer splits a cash deposit of ₹18 lakhs into three deposits of ₹6 lakhs each across different banks to avoid the reporting threshold of ₹10 lakhs. What type of transaction is this?"

Jagan: "Sir, this is an example of structuring, a tactic used to evade regulatory reporting requirements."

Interviewer: "Spot on. Cryptocurrencies are a trending topic these days. Can you name a few and share who regulates them in India?"

Jagan: "Popular cryptocurrencies include Bitcoin, Ethereum, and Dogecoin. Currently, India lacks a specific regulatory framework for cryptocurrencies, though they are not considered illegal."

Interviewer: "That's accurate. What is the range of a CIBIL score?"

Jagan: "CIBIL scores range from 300 to 900."

Interviewer: "Correct. Now let's assess your financial knowledge. If a loan applicant submits a balance sheet with current assets of ₹100 crores, non-current assets of ₹70 crores, current liabilities of ₹70 crores, and non-current liabilities of ₹50 crores, what would be the working capital?"

Jagan: "Sir, working capital is calculated as current assets minus current liabilities. In this case, it would be ₹100 crores minus ₹70 crores, resulting in ₹30 crores."

Interviewer: "Correct again. Moving to a more strategic perspective, how would you motivate your team if they are underperforming?"

Jagan: "Sir, understanding the root cause of underperformance is crucial. I would engage in one-on-one discussions with team members to address their concerns and provide targeted support. Regular training sessions, setting achievable goals, and recognizing their efforts can help in boosting morale and productivity.

Interviewer: "A thoughtful approach. Let's talk about the future of banking. What are your thoughts on the integration of artificial intelligence in banking operations?"

Jagan: "AI has immense potential to revolutionize banking. It can improve customer service through chatbots, enhance fraud detection, and optimize credit risk assessment. However, its implementation must be balanced with data privacy and regulatory compliance."

Interviewer: "Suppose a customer at your branch wants to apply for a Mudra loan but lacks the necessary documentation. How would you guide them?"

Jagan: "Sir, I would first educate the customer about the required documentation and assist them in obtaining the necessary papers. I'd also explore alternative means, such as leveraging local self-help groups or approaching the nearest Common Service Centre (CSC) for assistance."

Interviewer: "That's resourceful. What do you know about green banking, and how can banks contribute to environmental sustainability?"

Jagan: "Green banking involves practices that promote environmental sustainability. Banks can contribute by offering loans for renewable energy projects, implementing paperless banking, and promoting eco-friendly initiatives like green bonds."

Interviewer: "Impressive. Now, imagine a situation where a high-value customer threatens to close their account due to dissatisfaction. How would you handle it?"

Jagan: "I would listen to the customer's concerns attentively and assure them of prompt resolution. Depending on the issue, I'd involve relevant departments and ensure clear communication. Retaining such customers requires empathy, proactive solutions, and sometimes offering personalized benefits."

Interviewer: "A well-rounded answer. Finally, what's your vision for yourself in the next five years?"

Jagan: "Sir, I aspire to grow into leadership roles where I can drive strategic initiatives and mentor younger colleagues. I also aim to stay updated with emerging trends and continue contributing to the bank's success."

Interviewer: "That's inspiring, Jagan. Thank you for your responses so far and all the best for your promotion results."

• • •

CHAPTER IX

From Tamil Nadu to Andaman: A Credit Manager's Journey Through Isolation and Insight

Interview Snapshot - (Scale II to III)

This powerful interview with Arumuga Selvi reads like a field manual for rural credit officers and branch managers alike. Set against the backdrop of Andaman's unique banking terrain, it blends technical mastery with human-centered judgment. From navigating MSME classifications and fraud recovery to tackling infrastructure loans and policy shocks, Arumuga's responses are rich in insight and grounded in experience. Whether it's managing trust during crises or applying credit principles with empathy, this session offers practical wisdom, leadership clarity, and real-world scenarios that challenge even the most seasoned bankers.

Candidate Profile - Arumuga Selvi T (Manager, Scale II)

Arumuga Selvi T, a Scale II Manager with 8 years of banking experience, hails from Tamil Nadu and is currently posted in Diglipur, North Andaman. Specializing in the loans and advances section, he has developed strong expertise in credit appraisal, MSME financing, and customer relationship management. His remote posting has honed his adaptability and problem-solving skills, especially in resource-constrained environments. Known for his disciplined approach and dedication, Arumuga is committed to supporting financial inclusion while ensuring compliance and sound credit practices at the grassroots level.

• • •

Interviewer: "Congratulations, Mr. Arumuga Selvi, on clearing the written examination for the Scale III promotion. It's no small feat, especially considering your diverse experience across regions."

Arumuga Selvi: "Thank you, Sir. It's a privilege to be here today, and I appreciate this opportunity."

Interviewer: *[smiling slightly]* "I must say, it's intriguing to meet someone from Tamil Nadu posted in Diglipur, North Andaman. That's quite a leap geographically and culturally. How has this journey shaped you as a banker?"

Arumuga Selvi: "Indeed, Sir, it's been a transformative experience. The challenges were beyond just banking—adjusting to isolated geography, limited resources, and understanding the unique financial behaviors of island communities. But those very challenges refined my problem-solving abilities and adaptability."

Interviewer:*[nodding thoughtfully]* "Adaptability—a critical trait for leadership. Now, managing credit in mainland India is one thing, but how do you handle credit given to local fishermen in Diglipur, especially considering their fluctuating income patterns?"

Arumuga Selvi: "Sir, lending to fishermen requires a nuanced approach. We assess not just traditional financial documents but also consider seasonal earnings, weather patterns impacting their catch, and community references. We also encourage group guarantees, fostering a sense of shared responsibility."

Interviewer: *[raising an eyebrow with interest]* "Fascinating. Let's pivot a bit. Imagine this scenario: One of your long-standing fisherman clients, who has always maintained an excellent repayment record, suddenly defaults. Upon investigation, you discover he's been a victim of a fraudulent online investment scheme. What's your course of action?"

Arumuga Selvi: *[pausing briefly, then confidently]* "I'd start with empathy, recognizing his distress. Then, I'd explore restructuring options—perhaps a moratorium or rescheduling of payments—to ease his burden without compromising the bank's interests. Simultaneously, I'd guide him on filing a cyber fraud complaint, ensuring he receives proper legal support."

Interviewer:*[leaning back, impressed]* "That's a well-rounded approach. Now, shifting gears—let's talk technical. Can you explain the significance of a Garnishee Order and its implications on a customer's account?"

Arumuga Selvi: "Certainly, Sir. A Garnishee Order is issued by a court to attach the debtor's funds in the custody of a third party, often a bank. When we receive such an order, we're legally obligated to freeze the specified amount in the debtor's account, preventing any withdrawals until the court's directive is resolved."

Interviewer:*[quickly following up]* "Good. Moving on, under the Companies Act 2013, what's the importance of a 'One Person Company,' and how does it impact lending decisions?"

Arumuga Selvi: "A One Person Company allows a single individual to operate a corporate entity with limited liability. From a lending perspective, while it offers the legal protection of a company, credit decisions still heavily rely on the financial strength of that single promoter, making due diligence even more critical."

Interviewer: *[smiling slightly]* "Spot on. Now, let's spice things up. Suppose you're dealing with a property loan, and during verification, you discover that the title deed has been transferred multiple times within short intervals. How would you assess this under the Transfer of Property Act, 1882?"

Arumuga Selvi: "Sir, that would raise red flags for potential fraud or legal disputes. I'd scrutinize each transfer for authenticity, verify encumbrances through the sub-registrar, and demand a legal opinion to ensure the title is clear before proceeding."

Interviewer:*[leaning forward, intrigued]* "Excellent. Now, dealing with MSMEs is part of any credit manager's portfolio. How do you differentiate between a micro and a small enterprise when processing loans under the MSME framework?"

Arumuga Selvi: "Sir, as per the revised classification effective April 1, 2025, the distinction between micro and small enterprises is based on two key parameters: investment in plant and machinery or equipment, and annual turnover. A micro enterprise is defined as one with an investment up to ₹2.5 crore and turnover up to ₹10 crore. In contrast, a small enterprise can have an investment up to ₹25 crore and turnover up to ₹100 crore. These revised thresholds help accommodate the natural growth of MSMEs while still enabling them to benefit from targeted schemes."

Interviewer: "Impressive clarity. Now, ever encountered a situation where you had to apply factoring or forfaiting in your credit portfolio?"

Arumuga Selvi: "Yes, Sir. We facilitated a factoring arrangement for a local trader exporting spices. It allowed him to convert his receivables into immediate cash, improving his working capital without increasing debt."

Interviewer:*[raising an eyebrow]* "You're well-versed. Now, onto credit principles—what are the core principles that guide your credit management decisions?"

Arumuga Selvi: "Sir, the 5 Cs of credit—Character, Capacity, Capital, Collateral, and Conditions—form the bedrock of my approach. I always assess the borrower's intent, financial capacity, and external economic factors before sanctioning loans."

Interviewer:[*with a slight smirk*] "Since you brought up 'Character,' here's a personal one—what's the biggest character-defining moment you've experienced as a banker?"

Arumuga Selvi:[*after a brief pause*] "Sir, it was during the 2018 Andaman cyclone. Our branch was inundated, communication lines were down, and people needed urgent financial help. I organized community outreach, facilitated emergency loans without full documentation, and ensured basic banking services continued. It tested not just my professional skills but my moral compass."

Interviewer: [*visibly impressed*] "That's leadership in crisis. Now, a quick one—how do you detect early warning signs of an account slipping into NPA?"

Arumuga Selvi: "Sir, delayed payments, frequent cheque bounces, over-reliance on informal credit, sudden changes in business patterns, and poor stock turnover are key indicators. Regular monitoring and site visits are critical."

Interviewer: "Now, let's talk about something topical—how do you view the rise of digital lending platforms, and what risks do they pose to traditional banks?"

Arumuga Selvi: "Digital lending offers speed and accessibility but brings risks like data breaches, predatory lending, and regulatory gaps. Banks need to adopt fintech innovations while maintaining robust risk management frameworks."

Interviewer: [*leaning in*] "Last twist—imagine you're the Branch Head, and you discover that one of your officers has approved a fraudulent loan under your nose. What's your immediate course of action?"

Arumuga Selvi: [*firmly*] "I'd initiate an internal investigation, suspend the officer if necessary, and report the matter to higher authorities. Simultaneously, I'd start recovery proceedings to mitigate the bank's loss and ensure compliance with legal protocols."

Interviewer:[*leaning slightly forward, his tone shifting to a more reflective one*] "Mr. Selvi, let's dive into something many overlook in banking—the human side. Suppose you have a small business owner who's been a loyal customer for years. Suddenly, his business hits a rough patch, and he's unable to meet his loan obligations. His financials don't support restructuring, but you know his character well. Would you rely solely on the numbers, or does personal judgment play a role?"

Arumuga Selvi:*[pausing thoughtfully]* "Sir, while banking is data-driven, it's also deeply human. Financial statements tell one part of the story, but personal judgment fills the gaps numbers can't explain. I'd assess the feasibility of his business recovering through industry trends, perhaps consult local market dynamics, and evaluate if temporary relief measures could help. If I'm convinced of his intent and potential, I'd advocate for restructuring within regulatory norms. But yes, empathy balanced with prudence is key."

Interviewer: *[smiling faintly]* "Well said. Now, on a more technical note, can you walk me through how you would assess a proposal for a large infrastructure loan, considering risks associated with such projects?"

Arumuga Selvi:*[confidently]* "Certainly, Sir. Infrastructure loans come with complex risks—financial, operational, environmental, and regulatory. I'd begin with a detailed analysis of the project feasibility report, focusing on cost estimates, revenue models, and break-even analysis. Due diligence on promoters' track records, debt-equity ratio, and project cash flows is crucial. I'd stress-test the financials against adverse scenarios, assess political and environmental risks, and ensure proper legal clearances. Risk mitigation would involve robust covenants, escrow accounts, and adequate collateral."

Interviewer: *[raising an eyebrow, intrigued]* "Impressive depth. Now, a curveball to end with—if tomorrow, RBI introduces a sudden policy tightening, increasing repo rates significantly, how would that affect your loan portfolio, and what immediate actions would you take as a credit manager?"

Arumuga Selvi: *[without hesitation]* "Sir, an increase in repo rates would raise borrowing costs, potentially affecting borrowers' repayment capacities, especially in rate-sensitive sectors like MSMEs and real estate. I'd initiate a quick portfolio review to identify vulnerable accounts, particularly those with thin margins. Proactively engaging with such borrowers to reassess their repayment plans would be crucial. Simultaneously, I'd look to rebalance the portfolio by promoting products less sensitive to interest rate fluctuations. From a strategic standpoint, adjusting pricing models for new loans would also be necessary to maintain profitability."

Interviewer: *[leaning back, a reflective tone replacing the formal edge]* "You know, Mr. Selvi, interviews often test what candidates know. But today, you've shown not just knowledge but wisdom—the ability to connect policy with people, data with decisions, and risk with resilience."

(He pauses, then adds with a slight smile.)

"Banking isn't just about managing accounts; it's about managing trust. And from what I've heard today, you've not just balanced ledgers—you've balanced leadership with empathy. It's been a pleasure talking to you."

Arumuga Selvi: *[with a humble nod]* "Thank you, Sir. This conversation has been more than an interview—it's been a reflection of the journey we all undertake as bankers."

Interviewer:*[smiling genuinely]* "Indeed, Mr. Selvi. Best of luck—not just for the promotion, but for the impact you'll continue to make in every branch, every decision, and every life you touch."

• • •

CHAPTER X

From Credit Concepts to Customer Conflicts: How Zohra Jafaree Turned Setbacks into Strengths in Her Promotion Interview

Interview Snapshot - (Scale I to II)

This mock interview is a powerful example of growth, grace under pressure, and practical readiness. Zohra navigates setbacks with self-awareness, answers complex questions on banking guarantees, fraud handling, and financial literacy, and displays calm leadership in tense branch situations. Even when she answers incorrectly, her willingness to learn is evident. Her insights into customer education, OTS strategy, and guiding senior citizens on crypto highlight emotional intelligence and real-world application—making this interview a must-read for mastering both technical depth and human-centric banking.

Candidate Profile - Zohra Jafaree (Assistant Manager, Scale I)

Zohra Jafaree, a Scale I Officer originally from Surat, Gujarat, is currently posted in Ratnagiri, Maharashtra. Despite facing setbacks in the last three promotion exams and receiving modest appraisal scores, she remains determined and growth-oriented. A Certified Credit Professional, Zohra

• • •

Interviewer: "Good afternoon, Ms. Zohra Jafaree. First, let me congratulate you on making it to the interview stage once again. Your persistence is commendable."

Zohra: "Good afternoon, sir. Thank you very much. It's an honor to be here."

Interviewer: *[Leaning forward with a smile]* "So, Zohra, three attempts at promotion, and you're still here. Tell me, why do you think you haven't cleared the previous exams?"

Zohra: *[Pausing thoughtfully]* "Sir, I believe my failures were a result of misaligned preparation strategies. I focused heavily on theoretical concepts and neglected application-based scenarios, which form the crux of our day-to-day roles. But I've learned from these attempts, and this time, I've spent months sharping my practical knowledge and problem-solving skills. Failure taught me resilience and, more importantly, where I needed to improve."

Interviewer: *[Nodding approvingly]* "Zohra, sometimes, it's not about the setbacks but how you rise after them. Let's put your improved preparation to the test."

Interviewer: "You're a Certified Credit Professional, which is a strong credential. Let's talk about Incoterms 2020. Can you explain what DAP (Delivered at Place) means?"

Zohra: *[Confidently]* "Sir, DAP means that the seller delivers the goods at the buyer's premises, including unloading them."

Interviewer:*[Politely correcting]* "Not quite, Zohra. Under DAP, the seller delivers the goods ready for unloading at the agreed place of delivery. Unloading is the buyer's responsibility. This distinction is critical in avoiding disputes in international trade. Keep this in mind."

Zohra: "Thank you for clarifying, sir. I'll make a note of that."

Interviewer: *[Shifting gears]* "Now, imagine you're handling a particularly rowdy customer in your branch who is creating a ruckus over a failed transaction. How will you address the situation?"

Zohra: *[Calmly]* "Sir, in such situations, maintaining composure is crucial. First, I would invite the customer to a private space to de-escalate the public tension. Then, I'd listen patiently to his grievance, assuring him that his concern is being taken seriously. If possible, I'd resolve the issue immediately or provide a clear timeline for resolution. Throughout, I'd ensure that my tone is empathetic yet professional, making them feel heard and respected."

Interviewer: *[Impressed]* "Good. Handling irate customers with empathy is an art, and you seem to understand its importance."

Interviewer: "Cyber frauds are on the rise. As a branch manager, how would you educate your customers to prevent such incidents?"

Zohra: "Sir, I'd start with regular customer awareness programs, focusing on common fraud techniques like phishing, vishing, and SIM card swaps. Additionally, I'd ensure that our branch distributes educational materials highlighting secure banking practices, such as not sharing OTPs, PINs, or passwords. For our elderly customers, who are often the most vulnerable, I'd conduct one-on-one sessions or create simple videos in local languages. Social media could also be leveraged to reach a wider audience."

Interviewer:*[Encouragingly]* "That's a comprehensive approach, Zohra. Cybersecurity education must be relentless."

Interviewer: "What can you tell me about Deferred Payment Guarantees? How do they function?"

Zohra: *[Confidently]* "Sir, a Deferred Payment Guarantee is a commitment by a bank to pay installments over a specified period if the customer defaults. These guarantees are often used in credit sales of machinery or goods, ensuring the seller receives their due payments even if the buyer fails to honor their commitment."

Interviewer:*[Smiling]* "Well explained. Deferred Payment Guarantees play a vital role in securing trade."

Interviewer: "Let's talk about Nostro, Vostro, and Loro accounts. Can you briefly explain these terms?"

Zohra: "Certainly, sir. A Nostro account is our account in a foreign bank in their currency. A Vostro account is a foreign bank's account with us in our currency. A Loro account involves a third-party bank, where one bank refers to the account another bank holds with a foreign bank."

Interviewer:*[Nodding]* "Spot on. These accounts are foundational in international banking."

Interviewer: "You're posted in Ratnagiri, and I'm sure you encounter challenges unique to the region. Suppose a fisherman community seeks a collective loan but lacks formal collateral. How would you assess and process their application?"

Zohra:*[Thoughtfully]* "Sir, I'd leverage the SHG (Self-Help Group) or JLG (Joint Liability Group) model. These models allow for collective responsibility, ensuring repayment through peer accountability. Additionally, I'd assess their cash flow patterns during the fishing season and structure the loan repayment accordingly. Offering financial literacy sessions to the community would also be a priority, ensuring they understand their obligations."

Interviewer:*[Smiling]* "An innovative and empathetic approach. Well done."

Interviewer: "Next, Zohra, let's pivot to a lighter yet thought-provoking topic. If you were to describe your banking career in a single word, what would it be and why?"

Zohra:*[Smiling warmly]* "Sir, I'd say 'resilient.' This journey has been a series of challenges and learning opportunities, each making me stronger and more determined."

Interviewer: *[Leaning back with satisfaction]* "Resilient, indeed. I see that quality in your responses."

Interviewer: "Alright, Zohra, let's dive into some more complex scenarios before we wrap up. Here's the first one. A high-value corporate borrower has defaulted on its loan repayment. Despite several follow-ups, there is no sign of repayment. The company has offered to settle the loan through a one-time settlement (OTS) at 50% of the outstanding amount. How would you evaluate the proposal, considering the bank's financial health, NPA management, and regulatory compliance? Provide your decision-making approach."

Zohra:[*Pausing to think*] "Sir, in evaluating such an OTS proposal, I would follow a structured approach. First, I'd analyze the borrower's financials to assess their genuine inability to repay. I'd then evaluate the recoverability of the remaining 50% through other legal or recovery measures. If pursuing recovery appears uncertain or costly, I'd consider the OTS more favorably, especially if it can convert a high-value NPA into a performing asset.

Next, I'd review the bank's financial health—if the provisioning for this account is already high, accepting the OTS might immediately improve the profit and loss account. However, I'd ensure that the settlement aligns with regulatory compliance and internal policies to avoid any future scrutiny. Finally, I'd seek approval from the appropriate authority and document the justification thoroughly to maintain transparency."

Interviewer: [*Impressed*] "Good approach, Zohra. Balancing financial recovery and compliance is key in such decisions."

Interviewer: "Let's move to a situation you might encounter in your branch. A customer reports unauthorized transactions in their savings account amounting to   ₹5 lakh. The investigation reveals phishing as the root cause. How would you manage the customer's grievance, ensure compliance with the bank's fraud policy, and take measures to prevent similar incidents in the future?"

Zohra:[*Confidently*] "Sir, the first step is to empathize with the customer, assuring them that the matter is being taken seriously. I'd immediately freeze the account to prevent further unauthorized access and guide the customer on filing a formal complaint. Simultaneously, I'd escalate the case to the fraud management team for investigation and recovery.

In compliance with the bank's fraud policy, I'd analyze the timeline of the unauthorized transactions and assess the customer's negligence, if any. If the customer wasn't negligent, as per RBI guidelines, the bank would bear the liability, and I'd ensure the reimbursement is processed promptly.

To prevent such incidents, I'd enhance customer awareness through workshops and campaigns, educating them on recognizing phishing attempts. I'd also suggest implementing a branch-wide initiative to update customer contact details regularly and encourage multi-factor authentication for online banking."

Interviewer:*[Nodding in agreement]* "A comprehensive and customer-centric approach. Well done."

Interviewer:*[With a slight smile]* "One last question, Zohra. Suppose a senior citizen walks into your branch with a query about investing their savings in cryptocurrency. They're unsure about its safety and legitimacy. How would you counsel them?"

Zohra: *[Thoughtfully]* "Sir, I'd begin by acknowledging their interest and providing an unbiased overview of cryptocurrencies. I'd explain that while cryptocurrencies are gaining popularity, they remain unregulated in India, which exposes investors to significant risks such as price volatility and potential fraud. For a senior citizen relying on savings, I'd recommend exploring safer investment options like fixed deposits or government-backed schemes that offer steady returns.

At the same time, I'd highlight the importance of diversification and suggest seeking professional financial advice before making decisions. If they remain interested in cryptocurrencies, I'd stress the need for extreme caution and educate them about secure platforms and the risks involved."

Interviewer:*[Smiling]* "You've handled that diplomatically. Banking isn't just about transactions; it's about guiding customers wisely."

Interviewer:*[Leaning back, with a look of satisfaction]* "Zohra, you've done well today. You've demonstrated resilience, knowledge, and a problem-solving mindset. The panel appreciates your dedication. Before we conclude, do you have any questions for us?"

Zohra: *[Politely]* "Thank you, sir. I don't have any questions at the moment, but I'm grateful for this opportunity and the constructive feedback."

Interviewer: *[Warmly]* "You're welcome, Zohra. Keep up this spirit, and I'm sure success is around the corner. Best of luck for your promotion journey!"

• • •

CHAPTER XI

From Probation to Promotion: Gurjinder Singh's Journey to Scale 2 Leadership

Interview Snapshot (Scale I to II) -
This interview strikes the perfect balance between practical on-ground thinking and future-ready awareness. Gurjinder Singh's responses move seamlessly from handling rural connectivity outages and gold loan risks to decoding DeFi, money mules, and cryptocurrency volatility. What stands out is his ability to turn real branch challenges—like fraud attempts and demonetization pressure—into actionable insights. It's an interview packed with relatable scenarios, smart mitigation strategies, and calm confidence—ideal for anyone seeking to upgrade not just their answers, but also their approach to the interview table.

Candidate Profile- (Gurjinder Singh, Assistant Manager, Scale I)
Gurjinder Singh is a dedicated banking professional with 4 years of experience, having joined the industry as a Probationary Officer. Currently posted in Amritsar, he plays a key role in managing the credit section of the branch. Gurjinder brings strong expertise in branch operations, customer service, credit appraisal, and risk assessment. He has also demonstrated proficiency in NPA recovery, contributing significantly to asset quality improvement. Known for his analytical approach and operational efficiency, he is committed to delivering customer-centric solutions while maintaining regulatory compliance. His well-rounded skill set makes him a valuable asset in any credit and operations-focused banking role.

• • •

Interviewer: "Good morning, Mr. Gurjinder Singh. Congratulations on being shortlisted for the Scale 1 to Scale 2 promotion interview!"

Gurjinder: "Good morning, Sir. Thank you very much. I appreciate this opportunity."

Interviewer: "You have been working in the bank for the past four years, starting as a Probationary Officer. As you are now appearing for your first promotion interview, what do you think has been your biggest professional

58

growth during this period?"

Gurjinder: "Sir, during all these years, I have gathered a strong understanding of branch operations, customer service and compliance. For me, the biggest growth has been in terms of credit appraisal, risk assessment and handling of stressed assets. Also through the communication and reporting process for loan sanctioning, NPA recovery, and resolution of customer grievances, I have improved upon my decision making."

Interviewer: "That's a solid foundation. As a Scale 2 officer, you will have more responsibilities. Being posted in Amritsar, what's your way of handling gold loans at your branch, given the frequent fluctuation in gold prices?"

Gurjinder: "Sir, gold loans are a key part of our lending portfolio. We always use RBI-approved valuers because we comply with LTV (Loan-to-Value) guidelines. In order to manage the risk we analyse the gold price trends and do collateral review from time to time We also educate borrowers on timely payment of their dues so as to avoid overdue accounts. This is also useful for the profitability of the branch."

Interviewer: "Good. Let's say you are transferral to a region like South India where farmers are taking agricultural gold loans more often; what will be your approach?"

Gurjinder: "Respected Sir, people in South India take gold loans for agricultural purposes and repay them as per the harvest cycle. I would research regional patterns of agriculture, ensure that loans are utilized for agricultural purposes and keep track of repayments. Furthermore, I would stress on farmer awareness programmes for responsible borrowing."

Interviewer: "Well analyzed. Let us move to another scenario—namely when the demonetization happened in 2016, banks faced a significant operational challenge. According to your experience, what were the main challenges, how would you have handled them being a Scale 2 officer?"

Gurjinder: "Sir, demonetization led to long queues, customer frustration, and an increased risk of operational errors. Had I been a Scale 2 Officer, I would have ensured proper management of queues through issuing of tokens (the present scheme of managing queues is outdated). Further, there would have been dedicated counters for senior citizens along with proper communication regarding the withdrawal limits. Thereafter, I would guide my team to remain composed and efficient under pressure and follow RBI instructions."

Interviewer: "That's an effective approach. Coming to a recent event—there was a fraud attempt in your branch. Can you elaborate on what happened and how it was handled?"

Gurjinder: "Yes, Sir. A Customer tried to open a high-value savings account with forged KYC. The officers concerned found discrepancies in KYC during verification. We froze the account and notified senior management and other relevant authorities. Thanks to acting in time, we saved the bank from incurring substantial financial loss."

Interviewer: "That shows vigilance, which is essential for a Scale 2 officer. Let's discuss another operational challenge. You are managing a rural branch where there is no connectivity for five days & CBS transactions are not possible. How will you take care of customer expectations and operational issues?".

Gurjinder: "Sir, in such a situation, I would send a staff member to the nearest functioning branch to process urgent transactions. Especially cash transactions. I will ask the cashier to send the picture of cheque/withdrawal form to the staff member on whatsapp after duly verifying the physical presence of the customer. The staff member at other branch can verify the signature and post the payment in the system. Once done he can signal the cashier to make the payment. This is a bit time consuming but at least we can make the emergency payments."

Interviewer: "That's a very practical approach. Now, let's move to a technical question—what is the difference between pledged gold loans and hypothecated loans?"

Gurjinder: "Sir, in a pledged gold loan, the borrower hands over the gold to the bank as security, while ownership remains with the borrower. In a hypothecated loan, the asset (such as a vehicle or stock) remains in the borrower's possession, but the lender has a legal claim over it in case of default."

Interviewer: "Correct. As you know—cryptocurrencies have been a trending topic in finance. Do you think banks should accept cryptocurrencies as collateral?"

Gurjinder: "Sir, while cryptocurrencies have gained global traction, they are highly volatile and lack regulatory oversight in India. Given these risks, banks should avoid accepting them as collateral unless there is a well-defined regulatory framework. Risk mitigation is a top priority in banking, and without legal backing, such assets pose significant threats to financial stability."

Interviewer: "Gurjinder, financial inclusion remains a major challenge in India. In your view, what are the key obstacles banks face in achieving full financial inclusion?"

Gurjinder: "Sir, financial inclusion in India faces multiple challenges. One of the biggest issues is the penetration of bank branches into rural areas. Many rural locations are unviable due to high transaction costs and a fragmented population, which limits the scale of banking operations. To address this, we need to leverage technology and deploy a strong network of Business Correspondents (BCs). However, the current BC model is restrictive, with inadequate cash delivery points.

Another challenge is ensuring comprehensive participation from all stakeholders. Many financial inclusion programs rely on government and bank initiatives, but private sector collaboration is also necessary. In urban areas, the problem is different. Physical access is not the issue; instead, affordability and lack of proper identification for slum dwellers remain major concerns. Digital KYC solutions and affordable financial products could help overcome these issues."

Interviewer: "That's a well-rounded perspective. Moving on to another emerging trend—Decentralized Finance, or DeFi. Can you explain its significance in today's financial system?"

Gurjinder: "Certainly, Sir. DeFi, or Decentralized Finance, is a transformative development in the financial sector that utilizes blockchain and distributed ledger technology to offer financial services without the need for traditional intermediaries like banks. It enables lending, investing, and trading of digital assets through decentralized exchanges (DEXs).

The major advantage of DeFi is that it allows direct peer-to-peer transactions, reducing costs and increasing accessibility. It also promotes financial inclusion by offering services to people who might not have access to traditional banking. However, DeFi comes with risks, such as lack of regulation, security vulnerabilities in smart contracts, and potential misuse by bad actors. While DeFi is still evolving, its impact on the future of banking and finance cannot be ignored."

Interviewer: "That's an insightful response. Now, let's discuss financial fraud. Are you familiar with the term 'Money Mule'? How do they contribute to financial crime?"

Gurjinder: "Yes, Sir. A Money Mule is an individual who receives and transfers money on behalf of someone else, often without realizing they are facilitating financial fraud or money laundering. Criminal organizations use money mules to move illicit funds, making it harder for law enforcement to trace the money trail.

Money mules can be recruited through online job postings, social media scams, or even romance fraud, where someone is tricked into moving money for a so-called 'love interest.' In banking, it is crucial to educate customers and employees about this threat. Monitoring suspicious transactions, implementing stringent KYC norms, and conducting regular customer due diligence can help in identifying and preventing money mule activities."

Interviewer: "That's a very clear explanation. Now, to wrap up, why do you think you deserve this promotion, and how will you contribute to your new role as a Scale 2 officer?"

Gurjinder: "Sir, over the past four years, I have gained a deep understanding of banking operations, customer service, and risk management. I have consistently worked towards improving my knowledge, learning from past experiences, and adapting to new banking trends.

If promoted, I will focus on strengthening compliance, enhancing digital banking adoption among customers, and mentoring junior staff. I will also work towards improving financial inclusion in my branch and mitigating fraud risks through better monitoring and customer awareness. I am confident that my experience, dedication, and problem-solving abilities will allow me to excel in this role."

Interviewer: "That's great to hear, Gurjinder. You have demonstrated a strong understanding of banking, financial inclusion, digital finance, and risk management. Thank you for your time, and I wish you the best of luck for your promotion."

Gurjinder: "Thank you very much, Sir. It was a pleasure speaking with you.

• • •

CHAPTER XII

From Clerk to Change-Maker: The Inspiring Promotion Interview of a Specially-Abled Banker

Interview Snapshot - (Clerical to Scale I)

This inspiring interview with Pranith Banerjee showcases how dedication, adaptability, and continuous learning can overcome any obstacle—even physical limitations. From tackling real-world KYC challenges to mastering digital lending risks, his responses reflect strong leadership potential and operational awareness. His thoughtful approach to inclusivity, compliance, and customer service makes this a must-read for anyone preparing for their own banking promotion interview. A perfect blend of technical knowledge, human insight, and practical wisdom awaits inside.

Candidate Profile: Pranith Banerjee (Clerk)

Pranith Banerjee, currently serving as a clerk in Siliguri, is a dedicated and accomplished banking professional with a track record of delivering exceptional service. His primary responsibilities include savings account openings, passbook printing, cashier duties, and conducting meticulous Know Your Customer (KYC) verifications. Pranith has demonstrated a commitment to continuous learning by earning prestigious certifications like JAIIB, CAIIB, and Anti-Money Laundering by IIBF, equipping him with a strong foundation in banking operations and compliance.

Despite being specially-abled and wheelchair-bound, Pranith exemplifies resilience and adaptability, overcoming physical barriers to perform his duties with excellence. He is deeply committed to fostering inclusivity and improving accessibility in the workplace. Known for his empathetic approach, he ensures seamless customer experiences and adherence to regulatory norms. Soon to embark on a new chapter of his life with marriage, Pranith aspires to take on greater responsibilities as an officer, leveraging his skills to drive operational efficiency and customer satisfaction.

• • •

Interviewer: "Congratulations, Mr. Pranith Banerjee, on making it to the interview stage for the Clerical to Officer promotion. How are you feeling today?"

Pranith: "Thank you so much, Sir. I'm feeling excited and a bit nervous, but overall, I'm looking forward to the interaction."

Interviewer: "That's the right spirit, Pranith. Before we begin, let's talk a little about you. You've been serving as a clerk in Siliguri, right? Could you tell us about one memorable incident you've experienced at your branch?"

Pranith: "Certainly, Sir. One incident that stands out occurred last year when an elderly woman came to the branch for her first Aadhaar-linked account. She didn't speak much Hindi or English, and it was clear she was nervous. I noticed her hesitancy and offered to guide her personally. Step by step, I explained the process in simple terms and helped her complete all formalities. A week later, she returned with her grandson to thank me with a small box of sweets. It was heartwarming to see how such small efforts can make a significant impact on our customers."

Interviewer: "That's a lovely incident, Pranith. It shows your dedication to customer service. Now, I understand you are a specially-abled employee and use a wheelchair. What challenges have you faced in your role, and how have you overcome them?"

Pranith: "Sir, there have been challenges, especially when our branch facilities were not fully accessible. For example, accessing certain counters or dealing with files placed on high shelves required me to depend on colleagues. However, I've worked closely with my branch manager to identify areas of improvement. We now have ramps, and my workstation is designed for easier access. Personally, I've developed a system to handle tasks efficiently by leveraging digital tools whenever possible. Teamwork has been a big factor in overcoming these challenges."

Interviewer: "That's commendable. If given the opportunity to become an officer, what suggestions would you make to improve branch facilities for employees like yourself?"

Pranith: "Sir, I would suggest a comprehensive accessibility audit for the branch. Small but impactful changes like ergonomic furniture, accessible counters, and better signage can make a huge difference. Additionally, conducting regular sensitization workshops for staff to understand and support the needs of specially-abled colleagues would foster inclusivity."

Interviewer: "Excellent thoughts, Pranith. Let's shift gears a little. You handle KYC regularly in your current role. What steps do you follow to ensure accuracy and compliance while conducting KYC?"

Pranith: "Sir, I ensure that the documentation process strictly follows RBI guidelines. First, I verify the customer's identity proof and address proof thoroughly. I cross-check for any discrepancies in the documents. If it's a corporate account, I ensure all relevant resolutions and declarations are in order. Finally, I educate customers about the importance of KYC compliance to prevent future complications. For data entry, I double-check every detail before submission to avoid errors."

Interviewer: "That's a solid process. But tell me, how do you handle KYC for pardanishin women who may not feel comfortable providing their photographs or biometrics?"

Pranith: "Sir, I've come across such cases in Siliguri's culturally diverse environment. For pardanishin women, I ensure utmost respect and privacy. I arrange for a female colleague to handle biometric verification and other sensitive aspects in a private space. If that's not possible, I use certified alternative identification methods like Aadhaar OTP authentication or introducers as per KYC norms. I also ensure that they feel comfortable and are informed about the necessity of these steps."

Interviewer: "Very thoughtful, Pranith. Moving ahead, I notice you have certifications like JAIIB, CAIIB, and Anti-Money Laundering. While these are impressive, you don't have direct experience in credit or loans. How would you manage loan portfolios as an officer?"

Pranith: "Sir, I understand that credit management is a critical area for officers. While I don't have direct experience, I've started studying relevant materials, including RBI guidelines and loan policies. Additionally, I plan to enroll in the Certified Credit Professional course to gain specialized knowledge. On a practical level, I'd seek guidance from experienced officers and attend training sessions provided by the bank. I'm confident that my learning ability and certifications will help me adapt quickly to this responsibility."

Interviewer: "That's a proactive approach. Now, let's dive into a hypothetical scenario. Suppose a customer complains about being denied a loan despite fulfilling all eligibility criteria. How would you handle such a situation?"

Pranith: "Sir, I would first empathize with the customer and listen to their concerns without interrupting. Then, I'd review their application details to understand the reasons behind the rejection. If it was due to insufficient documentation or a misunderstanding, I'd guide them on how to rectify it. If the rejection was due to policy constraints, I'd explain it to them transparently and suggest alternative financial products or solutions. Maintaining transparency and offering alternatives would help resolve the issue amicably."

Interviewer: "Good approach. Now, let's test your banking knowledge. Can you tell me the key differences between NEFT and RTGS?"

Pranith: "Certainly, Sir. NEFT operates in half-hourly batches and is used for small-value transactions. There's no minimum limit, but there's a maximum limit depending on the bank. RTGS, on the other hand, is real-time and primarily for high-value transactions with a minimum limit of ₹ 2 lakh. NEFT can be used 24/7 now, thanks to recent upgrades, while RTGS is also available 24/7 as per the latest RBI guidelines."

Interviewer: "Correct. Here's another one. Recently, RBI has been focusing on digital lending. What do you think are the key risks associated with digital lending platforms?"

Pranith: "Sir, digital lending platforms often face risks such as data privacy breaches, lack of transparency in terms and conditions, high-interest rates, and unethical recovery practices. Additionally, there's the issue of regulatory arbitrage where unregulated entities exploit loopholes. RBI has introduced guidelines to address these, focusing on customer protection and stricter compliance measures."

Interviewer: "Well explained. Now, let's add a bit of a twist. Suppose you are managing a branch, and during a routine audit, a discrepancy in cash handling is identified. How would you address this issue as the branch manager?"

Pranith: "Sir, first, I'd review the audit findings thoroughly and identify the source of the discrepancy. Then, I'd cross-check with the cashier and other relevant staff to understand if it was a mistake or intentional. If it's a genuine error, I'd counsel the staff involved and ensure proper rectification. If there's suspicion of foul play, I'd report it to higher authorities and cooperate fully with the investigation. Simultaneously, I'd strengthen internal controls to prevent such incidents in the future."

Interviewer: "You've handled that well. Lastly, let's discuss Anti-Money Laundering. Can you explain what 'layering' means in the context of money laundering?"

Pranith: "Certainly, Sir. Layering refers to the process of disguising the origin of illicit funds by conducting complex transactions to separate the money from its criminal origin. This often involves multiple bank transfers, splitting funds into smaller amounts, or routing transactions through various jurisdictions to make tracing difficult."

Interviewer: "Spot on. One final question before we move ahead. Given your upcoming marriage, how do you plan to balance your personal and professional responsibilities as an officer?"

Pranith: "Sir, I believe that clear communication and time management are key. My fiancée is very supportive of my career goals, and we've already discussed strategies to balance our personal lives and my professional commitments. As an officer, I'd prioritize tasks effectively and ensure that I meet both professional and personal expectations without compromising on either."

• • •

CHAPTER XIII

How Gaurav Mastered Rural Branch Challenges and Aced His Promotion Interview

Interview Snapshot - (Clerical to Scale I)

Curious how to turn rural banking challenges into interview-winning stories? Gaurav's journey from Head Cashier to Scale 1 Officer is a goldmine of real-life problem-solving, smart compliance moves, and digital banking insights. This mock interview covers everything—from crisis management to cybersecurity and Open Banking—making it a must-read for any banker aiming for promotion. Get inspired by how practical experience and strategic thinking can make you stand out. Your Scale 1 success story could start here.

Candidate Profile: Gaurav Banerjee (Clerk)

Gaurav is a dedicated banking professional with five years of experience, currently serving as the Head Cashier in a rural branch. His role involves managing cash operations, ensuring compliance with regulatory requirements, and delivering exceptional customer service in a challenging rural setting. Gaurav has successfully cleared both JAIIB and CAIIB certifications, showcasing his strong foundation in banking principles and advanced knowledge in financial management and risk mitigation.

Hailing from Kolkata and currently posted in Haridwar, Gaurav has demonstrated resilience and adaptability in managing responsibilities far from home. His ability to balance operational excellence with a customer-focused approach makes him a strong contender for the Scale 1 Officer role. Known for his problem-solving skills and commitment to innovation, Gaurav is prepared to take on greater responsibilities and contribute meaningfully to the growth and success of his branch and the bank.

• • •

Interviewer: "Good morning, Mr. Gaurav, and congratulations on clearing the written examination for Scale 1 Officer."

Gaurav: "Good morning, Sir, and thank you very much!"

Interviewer: "First off, I see you're posted as a Head Cashier at a rural branch of Haridwar(Uttarakhand) district. Given that Haridwar is quite far from your hometown Kolkata, how do you manage staying so far from your family, and what motivates you to continue in this role?"

Gaurav: "Sir, being away from family has its challenges, but I am deeply committed to my work. The experience I've gained from working in a rural branch is unparalleled, and it motivates me to keep learning. The team here is like a second family, and over time, I've found a balance by visiting Kolkata during holidays. Plus, the role itself has taught me a lot about leadership and problem-solving."

Interviewer: "That's a great mindset, Gaurav. Now, since you are preparing for a Scale 1 Officer promotion, could you explain how your current role as Head Cashier prepares you for the responsibilities you'll take on as an officer?"

Gaurav: "As Head Cashier, I am responsible for managing cash transactions, ensuring compliance with regulatory requirements, handling large sums of money, and ensuring smooth operations in the cash department. This has taught me critical skills in financial management, attention to detail, and customer service. I believe these skills will be very relevant in the role of a Scale 1 Officer, where I'll need to manage both the financial and operational aspects of a branch."

Interviewer: "I see. You mentioned handling large sums of money. In a rural branch, cash handling can be tricky, especially when dealing with customer complaints or operational delays. Can you share an experience where you had to resolve a difficult cash-related issue and how you handled it?"

Gaurav: "Certainly, Sir. There was an instance when our branch faced a cash shortage due to a delay in the cash supply from the RBI. Customers were agitated as they had been waiting for their withdrawals. I immediately communicated the issue transparently, informing them about the delay. While managing their expectations, I made sure to prioritize withdrawals for those with urgent needs, and we arranged for a supplementary cash supply from a nearby branch. I also implemented a temporary solution where we allowed customers to deposit their cheques without any fees to alleviate the pressure. By the end of the day, the issue was resolved, and the customers were satisfied with how we handled the situation."

Interviewer: "That was a very practical approach, Gaurav. Now, let's talk about a more hypothetical scenario. Imagine your branch faces a sudden surge in customers due to a new government scheme. However, the internet connectivity is down, and you can't process digital transactions. How would you manage the situation?"

Gaurav: "Sir, this could be quite challenging, especially in a rural area where many people rely on digital channels for quick transactions. In this situation, I would first gather the customers and explain the technical issue. To prevent frustration, I'd ensure a fair system by prioritizing the most time-sensitive transactions, such as pension withdrawals or government benefit transfers. For others, we could take manual receipts and, once the internet is restored, process them in the system as soon as possible. Additionally, I'd set up a temporary counter for checking account balances, so customers aren't left in the dark. This will help maintain trust and ensure smooth operations until the connectivity issue is resolved."

Interviewer: "It seems you have thought through such scenarios. Now, as a Head Cashier, you're familiar with operational risks. Can you explain how you handle these risks, particularly in the context of cash handling and security?"

Gaurav: "Certainly, Sir. Operational risks in cash handling primarily involve issues such as cash shortages, fraud, or theft. To mitigate these risks, we maintain strict adherence to cash-handling procedures, including dual control for large cash deposits and withdrawals. At the start of every day, the cashier and I perform a thorough cash count. I also ensure that cash is stored in secure vaults with limited access. Regular audits are carried out to detect discrepancies, and we maintain a detailed record of every transaction. In case of discrepancies, we investigate immediately, liaise with the security team, and report the issue to higher authorities if needed. By adhering to these protocols, we minimize operational risks significantly."

Interviewer: "Good to know that you follow best practices, Gaurav. Let's now discuss a more contemporary topic—Open Banking. What do you understand by Open Banking, and how do you think it will impact Indian banking?"

Gaurav: "Open Banking, Sir, refers to the practice where banks share customer data with third-party service providers via secure APIs, but only with the customer's consent. This opens up the possibility of offering tailored financial products, like budgeting tools, account aggregation services, and quicker loan processing. For India, Open Banking could lead to a massive leap in digital banking, driving financial inclusion and increasing competition among banks and fintechs. It could also make banking more customer-centric, offering seamless, integrated services that cater to individual needs."

Interviewer: "That's a solid understanding, Gaurav. Given the rise of digital banking, we've seen a lot of fraudulent activities as well. Recently, there's been a surge in cases related to digital fraud. One of the prominent cases is the 'Digital Arrest' fraud. Can you elaborate on what this fraud is and how banks can protect themselves and customers from such incidents?"

Gaurav: "Yes, Sir. The 'Digital Arrest' fraud is a type of cybercrime where fraudsters pose as law enforcement or government officials. They typically call victims via video calls, claiming that the person is involved in illegal activities like money laundering or narcotics trafficking. The fraudsters then pressure the victim into transferring money to a so-called 'safe government account' for investigation or verification purposes. Sometimes, they even use forged documents and display fake badges to appear authentic.

This is not about fake banking apps, but rather a psychological scam exploiting fear and authority. To prevent such frauds, banks and authorities should increase public awareness about such tactics, advise customers never to share personal details or transfer money under pressure, and promote reporting such incidents to cybercrime cells. Digital literacy and timely alerts via SMS or social media can play a key role in prevention."

Interviewer: "Excellent. You've mentioned customer education multiple times. How do you think this can be implemented in rural areas, where many people may not be well-versed in digital banking?"

Gaurav: "In rural areas, Sir, face-to-face education is crucial. We can organize awareness camps, where we demonstrate safe digital banking practices. It's important to use local languages and simple terms so that everyone understands. We can also distribute leaflets, put up posters in branches, and even use local influencers, such as village heads, to reinforce the message. Additionally, we can educate customers on the importance of safeguarding their PINs and the risks of sharing personal information over the phone or online."

Interviewer: "That's a great approach. Let's shift gears a bit. I see you've cleared both JAIIB and CAIIB. How do you think these certifications have helped in your career so far?"

Gaurav: "Sir, both certifications have enhanced my understanding of banking concepts significantly. JAIIB laid the foundation for core banking knowledge, while CAIIB helped me dive deeper into risk management, treasury, and financial analysis. These certifications have not only helped me improve my performance in day-to-day operations but have also given me a strategic mindset that I believe will be beneficial in my next role as a Scale 1 Officer."

Interviewer: "That's great to hear. Now, in your opinion, what are the key financial ratios or metrics that a branch manager should keep an eye on to ensure healthy financial operations?"

Gaurav: "Some of the key metrics include the Net Interest Margin (NIM), which indicates how efficiently the bank is utilizing its assets to generate income. The Cost-to-Income ratio is another important one, as it reflects the bank's operational efficiency. I'd also focus on the Non-Performing Assets (NPA) ratio, which directly affects the health of the loan portfolio. Additionally, liquidity ratios, such as the Cash Reserve Ratio (CRR) and the Liquidity Coverage Ratio (LCR), would be critical to monitor for maintaining the branch's financial stability."

Interviewer: "You've been thorough in your answers, Gaurav. Let me now present a scenario that tests your decision-making skills. Suppose you receive information about a large structuring transaction being carried out by one of your regular customers. What steps would you take to address this issue?"

Gaurav: "Sir, if I found that a customer was structuring their transactions, I would immediately report it to the bank's anti-money laundering team. I would ensure that the transaction is flagged and review any other related transactions for further suspicious activity. As per the bank's AML policies, I would also file a Suspicious Transaction Report (STR) to the Financial Intelligence Unit. My role here would be to ensure all compliance procedures are followed, and I would work with the relevant teams to ensure the issue is fully investigated."

Interviewer: "That's a very professional approach, Gaurav. You've displayed strong knowledge and a great deal of practical insight. I'm confident that you're ready for this promotion. Let's continue with a few more questions to wrap things up."

Interviewer: "Let's move to another important topic, Gaurav. As you know, the banking industry is moving towards a cashless economy, especially with the rise of UPI and digital wallets. How do you think this shift affects rural branches like yours, and how would you prepare your team for such a transition?"

Gaurav: "Sir, the shift towards a cashless economy has both opportunities and challenges for rural branches. On one hand, it reduces the dependency on physical cash, which can ease operational load and improve security. On the other hand, the lack of digital literacy and infrastructure in rural areas makes adoption slow. To prepare for this transition, I would focus on training my team to handle digital transactions effectively and educate customers about the benefits and safety of digital payments. This could include setting up help desks in the branch, conducting workshops, and even using success stories to motivate customers. Ensuring robust infrastructure, like uninterrupted internet and power, would also be a priority."

Interviewer: "That's a thoughtful approach. Speaking of infrastructure, let's discuss cybersecurity. Suppose a customer reports an unauthorized UPI transaction from their account. What steps would you take to assist them?"

Gaurav: "Sir, in such a situation, I would first calm the customer and assure them of our assistance. Then, I'd immediately block the customer's UPI account to prevent further transactions. Next, I'd help them file a formal complaint and guide them through the process of raising a dispute with our bank. Simultaneously, I'd escalate the matter to our IT and fraud investigation teams. We would also check the transaction logs to identify the source of the fraud and take corrective measures. Finally, I'd ensure the customer receives updates on the progress of the investigation and any reimbursement, if applicable."

Interviewer: "Good. Now let's test your awareness of recent banking regulations. RBI recently announced measures to improve the efficiency of loan processing in rural branches. Can you highlight any such recent initiatives?"

Gaurav: "Yes, Sir. One recent initiative is the introduction of the Account Aggregator (AA) framework, which aims to simplify the loan approval process by allowing banks to access a customer's financial data in a consent-based and secure manner. This reduces the dependency on physical documents and speeds up decision-making. Additionally, the Kisan Credit Card (KCC) digitization program has streamlined the process for farmers to access credit, ensuring faster disbursal and better monitoring."

Interviewer: "Very good. Let's shift gears slightly. Since you mentioned risk earlier, let me ask you this: How would you handle a situation where one of your team members is found bypassing standard cash-handling procedures, leading to a discrepancy in the accounts?"

Gaurav: "Sir, this is a serious issue that needs to be addressed with both caution and fairness. First, I would investigate the matter thoroughly by reviewing the records and speaking to the concerned team member to understand their perspective. If it's found to be an error, I'd ensure proper training to avoid future lapses. However, if the act is intentional, I'd escalate it to higher authorities as per the bank's disciplinary procedures. At the same time, I'd conduct a branch-wide refresher session on cash-handling protocols to reinforce the importance of compliance and accountability."

Interviewer: "That's a balanced approach. Since you are already preparing for a Scale 1 role, let me ask you a question that tests your understanding of branch management. What steps would you take to improve a rural branch's profitability?"

Gaurav: "Sir, improving the profitability of a rural branch requires a deep understanding of the local economy and community needs. First, I'd focus on increasing the CASA base by organizing financial literacy camps in villages, targeting SHGs, panchayats, and local traders. Second, I'd actively promote government-sponsored schemes like PMJJBY, PMSBY, and APY, which are well-received in rural areas and help in fee-based income. Third, I'd ensure credit is extended responsibly under schemes like KCC, PMEGP, and Mudra Loans, while also strengthening recovery mechanisms through regular follow-ups and local-level coordination. Lastly, I'd build strong grassroots relationships by participating in gram sabhas and village events, positioning our branch as a trusted partner in rural development."

Interviewer: "That's an excellent strategy. Now, let's discuss your certifications. As a CAIIB-qualified professional, you must be familiar with Treasury Management. Can you explain how Treasury contributes to a bank's profitability?"

Gaurav: "Yes, Sir. Treasury plays a crucial role in managing a bank's liquidity, investments, and risks. By efficiently managing the bank's funds, treasury ensures that surplus funds are invested in high-yielding instruments, contributing to profitability. It also manages interest rate and forex risks through hedging and arbitrage strategies. Additionally, treasury operations like government securities trading and interbank lending help generate revenue while maintaining regulatory compliance."

Interviewer: "Good. Since we're discussing risk management, let me pose another scenario. Imagine a customer insists on withdrawing ₹10 lakh in cash, claiming it's for a business purpose. However, the transaction seems suspicious, and you're unsure if it complies with AML norms. How would you handle this?"

Gaurav: "Sir, in such a situation, I'd politely request the customer to provide supporting documentation for the withdrawal, such as an invoice or purchase order, to ensure the legitimacy of the transaction. If the customer cannot provide satisfactory proof, I'd flag the transaction for further review and report it to the bank's AML team as a precautionary measure. Meanwhile, I'd also educate the customer on the risks of handling large amounts of cash and suggest alternative methods like RTGS/NEFTs or demand drafts."

Interviewer: "That's a prudent response. Let's conclude with one final question, Gaurav. Given your rural branch experience, what's one innovation you think could revolutionize banking in rural India?"

Gaurav: "Sir, one innovation that could revolutionize rural banking is the widespread adoption of biometric-based banking services. With Aadhaar already being a cornerstone of identity in India, integrating biometric authentication into banking transactions can make financial services more accessible and secure for rural customers. This would eliminate the need for passwords or PINs, which many customers find challenging, and ensure inclusivity, even for those who are less literate."

Interviewer: "That's a great insight, Gaurav. I can see that you have a clear understanding of banking operations and a strong commitment to your role. Let's wrap it up here for now, but I look forward to seeing you excel in your new role soon."

• • •

CHAPTER XIV

From Rural Roots to Rising Roles: How Ramesh Tackled Tricky Scenarios in Promotion Interview and Impressed the Panel

Interview Snapshot - (Scale I to II)

This engaging mock interview showcases how to respond thoughtfully to real-life branch management dilemmas, tricky HR scenarios, and policy-related questions. From handling sensitive staff issues to negotiating with landlords and dealing with demanding customers, Ramesh demonstrates the right mix of empathy, practicality, and presence of mind. His approach to rural lending, financial inclusion, and credit assessment adds strong technical depth. A must-read for sharpening situational judgment, improving answer structure, and learning how to turn challenges into opportunities during the interview.

Candidate Profile: Ramesh (Assistant Manager, Scale I)

Ramesh is a dynamic and dedicated banker with three years of experience at a leading public-sector bank. During his tenure, he has excelled in customer service, credit analysis, and operational efficiency. Ramesh began his career with a strong foundation, clearing the JAIIB in his first year, and is now pursuing both CAIIB certification and an MBA from IGNOU, showcasing his commitment to continuous learning.

His time at a rural branch has honed his problem-solving skills and deepened his understanding of grassroots-level banking. He has effectively managed customer relationships, streamlined branch operations, and contributed to improving recovery rates in challenging scenarios.

Known for his adaptability and team-oriented approach, Ramesh views transfers as opportunities for growth and cross-cultural exposure. His keen interest in financial inclusion and innovative banking solutions makes him a valuable asset to the institution, ready to take on larger responsibilities with confidence.

• • •

Interviewer: "Congratulations, Ramesh, for clearing the written exam! Your scores are quite impressive."

Ramesh: "Thank you very much, sir. I've worked hard for this opportunity."

Interviewer: "That's commendable, Ramesh. You've completed three years in the bank, correct? What has been the most memorable moment of your banking career so far?"

Ramesh: "Yes, sir, I have completed three years. While each day has offered unique lessons, my most memorable moment was my very first day at the bank. Walking in as an employee instead of a customer was a proud and transformative experience. Sitting behind the counter and serving customers was a moment that will stay with me forever."

Interviewer: "A significant milestone indeed. I hope you achieve even greater milestones as you progress. Now, Ramesh, after this promotion, you may be posted anywhere in the country. How do you feel about being transferred to a remote region, say South India or the North-East?"

Ramesh: "Sir, I am fully prepared for such a posting. Being a bachelor, I have minimal personal responsibilities and view this as an opportunity to broaden my horizon. Banking in different regions will help me understand diverse customer profiles and enhance my adaptability. I am ready to take on any challenge that comes with the transfer."

Interviewer: "Good attitude, Ramesh. That kind of flexibility is essential for success in our field. I noticed you cleared JAIIB in your first year. Why haven't you cleared CAIIB yet?"

Ramesh: "Sir, I attempted CAIIB during my first year, but unfortunately, demonetization occurred around the same time. The workload was immense, and I couldn't prepare adequately for the December exams. Subsequently, I enrolled in an MBA program at IGNOU, and my semester exams often clashed with CAIIB schedules. However, I've applied for the upcoming June attempt and am determined to clear it this time."

(If you have not cleared JAIIB/CAIIB then prepare for this question really well)

Interviewer: "I appreciate your honesty, Ramesh. Balancing multiple commitments is challenging. Best of luck with your MBA and CAIIB. Let's shift gears now. Imagine you are the branch manager, and one of your assistants consistently arrives late, citing her husband's serious illness as the reason. Customers have begun complaining. She's hardworking and intelligent, but her tardiness is becoming a concern. How would you handle this?"

Ramesh: "Sir, this is a sensitive matter that requires empathy and practicality. I would first have a one-on-one discussion with her to understand the full extent of her situation. If her circumstances demand flexibility, I'd explore solutions such as staggered work hours or assigning her to back-office duties that don't require direct customer interaction. I would also encourage her colleagues to support her during this difficult time. Such measures would ensure smooth branch operations while demonstrating compassion and solidarity."

Interviewer: "That's a thoughtful approach. Now, let's move to a broader issue. Recently, several state governments announced farm loan waivers. What is your opinion on their impact on the banking sector?"

Ramesh: "Sir, in my opinion, farm loan waivers provide temporary relief but have long-term negative consequences. They disrupt credit discipline among borrowers, especially in rural areas. Farmers begin to anticipate waivers, which affects repayment behavior. I've observed this firsthand in my rural branch. Recovery efforts become increasingly difficult as borrowers assume that their loans will eventually be written off."

Interviewer: "But Ramesh, wouldn't waivers reduce NPAs and provide immediate relief to banks?"

Ramesh: "While it's true that waivers may temporarily reduce NPAs, they don't address the root cause of the issue. Accounts cleared under waivers often fall back into default over time. A more sustainable solution would involve offering interest subsidies or providing farmers with resources like better Minimum Support Prices (MSPs) and affordable inputs to increase their income. This would empower them to repay loans without external interventions."

Interviewer: "A well-argued perspective. Let's turn to a hypothetical case. Suppose a homemaker named Smt. Radha, who owns four flats in Trivandrum and earns a monthly rental income of ₹50,000, visits your branch. She urgently needs ₹10 lakhs for her daughter's wedding. How would you assist her?"

Ramesh: "Sir, I would suggest a personal loan against the mortgage of her immovable property. After verifying her eligibility, including her CIBIL score and property valuation, I would process the loan application. Assuming her self-occupied property is valued at ₹20 lakhs, a loan of ₹10 lakhs could be safely sanctioned, provided all documentation and eligibility criteria are met."

Interviewer: "That's a precise response. Now, tell me, Ramesh, what is the interest rate on the Reserve Bank of India's latest Repo Rate?"

Ramesh:[*Pauses*] "Sir, I'm afraid I don't have the exact figure at the moment."

Interviewer: "That's unexpected, Ramesh. Isn't it crucial for a banker to be aware of such key statistics?"

Ramesh: "You are absolutely right, sir. It's an oversight on my part, and I take full responsibility for it. I regularly follow monetary updates, but I must have missed this one. I will ensure I double-check such figures daily, so I'm always prepared."

Interviewer: "Fair enough, Ramesh. How would you prevent such knowledge gaps as a branch manager?"

Ramesh: "Sir, I would introduce a daily briefing session at the branch where key updates, such as policy rates and regulatory changes, are shared with the team. This practice would ensure collective awareness and help us stay prepared for customer queries."

Interviewer: "A proactive approach. Let's discuss another hypothetical situation. Suppose your branch's lease is expiring, and the landlord insists on building a multiplex above the premises. He demands a 'No Objection' certificate for this or a steep rent hike from ₹50,000 to ₹1,50,000 with a 15% annual increase. How would you handle this?"

Ramesh: "Sir, constructing a multiplex above a bank poses serious security risks and could deter customers. I would first try to negotiate with the landlord, explaining the potential impact on the branch's operations. If he remains adamant, I would involve higher authorities and mutual acquaintances to mediate. Meanwhile, I would scout for alternative premises to ensure business continuity and explore the possibility of the bank paying a reasonable market rent within policy limits."

Interviewer: "Good thinking, Ramesh. Let's discuss the Kisan Samman Nidhi scheme announced in the budget. How much is the first installment that farmers will receive?"

Ramesh: "Sir, under the Kisan Samman Nidhi scheme, farmers owning up to 2 hectares of cultivable land are entitled to ₹6,000 annually. The first installment of ₹2,000 has already been disbursed."

Interviewer: "Accurate. Here's a scenario to test your problem-solving skills. Suppose your branch's loan portfolio has a high percentage of NPAs. As the manager, what measures would you take to address this?"

Ramesh: "Sir, my first step would be to analyze the portfolio and identify patterns in defaults. Based on these insights, I would prioritize recovery efforts for accounts with the highest chances of repayment. I would also strengthen pre-sanction credit appraisals and post-disbursement monitoring. Educating borrowers about timely repayment and offering restructuring options to genuine cases would be integral parts of my strategy."

Interviewer: "An effective approach. Now, Ramesh, imagine a corporate client approaches your branch seeking a cash credit facility of ₹50 crores. However, their financials show declining profits over the past three years. How would you assess the proposal?"

Ramesh: "Sir, I would thoroughly evaluate their financial statements, focusing on cash flow, debt levels, and repayment capacity. Declining profits raise red flags, so I would seek additional collateral and guarantees. I would also assess their industry's growth potential and any external factors impacting their performance before making a decision."

Interviewer: "Good, Ramesh. One last question. If you were given a choice to introduce a new product in the bank, what would it be and why?"

Ramesh: "Sir, I would propose a customized savings-cum-loan product for rural areas. This product would encourage financial inclusion by allowing small savings to accumulate as collateral for micro-loans. Such a product would address the credit needs of underserved communities while promoting savings habits."

Interviewer: "That's innovative, Ramesh. Thank you for your insightful responses today. Best of luck with your promotion."

Ramesh: "Thank you, sir. It's been an honor to discuss these topics with you. Have a great day!"

• • •

CHAPTER XV

Navigating Treasury, Compliance, and Crisis: A Scale III Interview Packed with Practical Banking Insight

Interview Snapshot - (Scale II to III)

This mock interview is a goldmine for understanding Treasury operations through real-world scenarios. It dives deep into liquidity crunch responses, foreign exchange risk management, interest rate swaps, and arbitrage strategies. Sunil also navigates complex legal distinctions, like garnishee vs. attachment orders and Section 20 of the NI Act, with precision. His thoughtful responses to certification gaps and banking mergers show maturity and strategic thinking. This is a must-read for mastering technical concepts, legal acumen, and structured, confident responses expected at the Scale 2 to 3 level.

Candidate Profile - Sunil Meena (Manager, Scale II, Treasury Department)

Sunil Meena, a native of Churu (Rajasthan), is currently serving as a Scale II Officer in the Treasury Department of a leading bank, posted in Delhi. With an MBA in Finance, he brings a strong academic foundation and practical exposure to core treasury functions such as liquidity management, investment operations, and forex dealings. Known for his analytical mindset and calm composure under pressure, Sunil has developed a keen understanding of banking regulations and market dynamics. Though he hasn't cleared JAIIB and CAIIB yet, his hands-on treasury experience and grasp of legal and financial knowledge make him a well-rounded banking professional.

• • •

Interviewer: "Good morning, Mr. Meena, and congratulations on being shortlisted for the Scale III promotion interview!"

  Sunil Meena: "Good morning, sir. Thank you very much. It's an honor to be here."

Interviewer: "The honor is ours to have someone from Churu, Rajasthan, now working in the bustling Treasury Department in Delhi. Quite a leap! Before we dive into banking, how has your journey been from Churu to Delhi?"

Sunil Meena: *[smiling]* "Thank you, sir. It has been an exciting and enriching journey. Growing up in Churu instilled in me a strong work ethic and adaptability, which have helped me navigate the complexities of working in a high-pressure environment like Treasury in the heart of Delhi."

Interviewer: *[nodding thoughtfully]* "Interesting. But I noticed you haven't cleared your JAIIB or CAIIB certifications yet, which could have added to your professional edge. Why the delay?"

Sunil Meena: "Yes, sir, that's a valid point. My primary focus has been on mastering Treasury operations and pursuing my MBA in Finance. With these demanding roles, I couldn't prioritize JAIIB or CAIIB. However, I have recently enrolled in JAIIB and plan to clear CAIIB subsequently."

Interviewer: *[raising an eyebrow]* "A fair answer, but remember, certifications are crucial in adding value to your profile. Moving on, Treasury is a critical function. Can you explain how banks manage foreign exchange risk in the Treasury Department?"

Sunil Meena: *[leaning forward]* "Certainly, sir. Banks use various tools like forward contracts, currency swaps, and options to hedge against foreign exchange risk. Additionally, active monitoring of market trends and maintaining sufficient reserves in different currencies helps mitigate risks associated with currency fluctuations."

Interviewer: "Good. Now, let's discuss liquidity management in Treasury. What are the key strategies to ensure sufficient liquidity while maximizing returns?"

Sunil Meena: "Sir, ensuring liquidity involves maintaining an optimal balance between cash reserves and investments in liquid assets. Strategies include repo and reverse repo transactions, interbank borrowing, and active portfolio management of short-term government securities. Additionally, monitoring cash flow projections and regulatory liquidity ratios like LCR and NSFR is critical."

Interviewer: *[smiling approvingly]* "Impressive. Now, let me challenge you with a different angle—what's your perspective on the recent wave of mergers in the banking sector?"

Sunil Meena: *[pausing briefly]* "Sir, while mergers enhance operational efficiency and scale, they also pose integration challenges, such as aligning cultures and systems. For example, the recent mergers among public sector banks have improved capital adequacy and operational synergy but require continuous efforts in staff training and technological integration to be fully effective."

Interviewer: *[leaning back]* "That's spot on. Now, let's take a step back to legal concepts. Explain the statement: 'A minor cannot become a partner but can be admitted to the benefits of a partnership firm."

Sunil Meena: *[confidently]* "Sir, a minor, due to lack of contractual capacity, cannot be a partner but can be admitted to the benefits of a partnership. On attaining majority, they must decide within six months whether to continue or leave the partnership. If they remain silent, they are deemed a full partner from the beginning and liable for the firm's acts. Moreover, they cannot stop payment of cheques issued by the firm."

Interviewer: "Correct. Let's explore garnishee orders versus attachment orders. What is the difference?"

Sunil Meena: "Sir, the primary difference lies in their issuance and scope. A garnishee order is issued by a court of law and applies only to the balance available in an account at the time of receipt of the order, excluding future credits. On the other hand, an attachment order is issued by revenue authorities and covers both the existing balance and future credits in the account.

In terms of applicability, a garnishee order is valid only when the relationship between the bank and the customer is that of debtor and creditor. Meanwhile, an attachment order applies regardless of the relationship and can also cover future liabilities."

Interviewer: "Excellent. Let's touch upon the NI Act. Can you elaborate on Section 20 regarding inchoate instruments?"

Sunil Meena: "Sure, sir. An inchoate instrument is incomplete, with details like date, payee, or amount left blank. Under Section 20 of the Negotiable Instruments Act, the holder has the right to complete the instrument, provided it does not amount to material alteration. This flexibility ensures negotiability while protecting the holder's interests."

Interviewer: "Sunil, Treasury has its challenges, but what do you see as the biggest challenge in today's banking landscape?"

Sunil Meena: "Sir, digitization is both a boon and a challenge. While it enhances efficiency, it increases exposure to cyber risks. Balancing innovation with stringent cybersecurity measures is, in my view, the biggest challenge."

Interviewer:[*leaning forward, intrigued*] "Before we wrap up, here's a hypothetical situation. Suppose the Treasury faces a liquidity crunch just before closing hours, and the interbank market is non-responsive. How would you handle it?"

Sunil Meena:[*after a thoughtful pause*] "Sir, in such a scenario, I would first assess internal sources like callable deposits or surplus liquidity across branches. Simultaneously, I'd explore overnight lending options with trusted counterparts. If these fail, using the Marginal Standing Facility as a last resort could provide immediate relief."

Interviewer:[*with a smile of approval*] "Impressive thinking under pressure! Let's pivot to a technical concept. In Treasury operations, managing interest rate risk is critical. Can you explain how a bank uses Interest Rate Swaps (IRS) to hedge against fluctuations in interest rates?"

Sunil Meena:[*with a composed smile*] "Certainly, sir. An Interest Rate Swap (IRS) is a derivative contract where two parties exchange interest payment obligations on a notional principal. Typically, one party pays a fixed rate while the other pays a floating rate, such as LIBOR or MIBOR.

Banks use IRS to hedge interest rate risks by stabilizing their cost of funds or returns on assets. For instance, if a bank has issued floating-rate loans but its funding is fixed-rate, it can enter an IRS to convert its fixed-rate liability into a floating one, thus matching its asset-liability profile and reducing exposure to interest rate volatility."

Interviewer: "Excellent, Sunil. That's a well-articulated response!"

Interviewer:[*leaning forward, intrigued*] "Sunil, let's talk about the current financial markets. In Treasury, managing liquidity is as critical as managing risks. How do banks use Certificate of Deposits (CDs) as a tool for liquidity management?"

Sunil Meena: "Sir, Certificates of Deposit are short-term instruments issued by banks to manage liquidity. When a bank anticipates a shortfall in funds, it can issue CDs to raise capital quickly from institutional investors. CDs are attractive due to their fixed interest rates and short maturity periods, typically ranging from 7 days to one year.

Additionally, CDs allow banks to diversify their funding sources and manage liquidity gaps without relying entirely on interbank markets or repo agreements. They are also tradable in secondary markets, enhancing flexibility in liquidity management."

Interviewer: [*nodding in approval*] "Good. Now, Treasury is often at the center of a bank's profit-making activities. Can you explain the role of

Treasury in arbitrage opportunities, especially in the forex market?"

Sunil Meena: *[smiling confidently]* "Certainly, sir. Treasury exploits arbitrage opportunities by leveraging differences in currency values or interest rates across markets. For example, in the forex market, a bank's Treasury may engage in triangular arbitrage, buying and selling currencies across three different pairs to capitalize on inefficiencies in exchange rates.

Similarly, in the interest rate market, Treasury can use carry trades, borrowing in a low-interest currency and investing in a higher-yielding currency. These strategies require meticulous risk assessment and swift execution to ensure profitability while staying compliant with regulatory norms."

Interviewer:*[raising an eyebrow for a final challenge]* "Interesting. Lastly, Sunil, let's test your understanding of derivatives further. Can you explain the concept of a Non-Deliverable Forward (NDF) and its relevance in emerging markets like India."

Sunil Meena: "Sir, a Non-Deliverable Forward is a derivative contract used for hedging or speculating on currencies that are not freely convertible, such as the Indian Rupee. Unlike a traditional forward contract, an NDF is settled in cash rather than through physical delivery of the currency.

The settlement amount is determined by the difference between the agreed exchange rate and the prevailing spot rate on the settlement date. NDFs are highly relevant in emerging markets as they allow international investors and corporations to hedge currency risks without violating local currency regulations."

Interviewer: *[with a satisfied smile]* "Sunil, your grasp of Treasury concepts is commendable. You've demonstrated not just technical knowledge but also the ability to apply it practically. One final piece of advice: as you progress in your career, stay updated with emerging trends like CBDCs and sustainability-linked financing. They are shaping the future of Treasury operations."

Sunil Meena:*[with a smile]* "Thank you, sir. I truly appreciate the guidance and this opportunity to showcase my knowledge."

Interviewer: "We wish you the best for your promotion, Sunil. Keep up the good work, and I'm sure you'll make a significant impact in your next role."

Sunil Meena: "Thank you, sir. I'll strive to live up to the expectations."

• • •

86

Crisis, Compliance, and Clarity: A Scale 4 Mock Interview That Showcases Real Banking Brilliance

Interview Snapshot - (Scale III to IV)

Packed with rich field experience and strategic clarity, this interview with Arijit Dasgupta offers much more than textbook answers. It explores real scenarios—from cyber-attacks and rural loan defaults to managing forex risk and financial literacy in low-trust regions. Arijit's thoughtful handling of tough questions on DSCR, Letters of Credit, and market volatility reveals both depth and maturity. His academic pursuit of a PhD and aspiration to teach make this a compelling blueprint for those aiming to blend hands-on banking excellence with leadership vision.

Candidate Profile - Arijit Dasgupta (Senior Branch Manager, Scale III)

Arijit Dasgupta, a seasoned banker with a rich experience spanning West Bengal, Bihar, and Assam, is currently posted as a Senior Branch Manager (Scale 3) in Tinsukia. Originally from Malda, West Bengal, Arijit has successfully led rural and urban branches across diverse geographies. He has been recognized as Best Branch Manager three times for his exceptional leadership and performance. At 45, his passion for learning remains strong—he is currently pursuing a PhD in Management. With a long-term goal of becoming an instructor at the Bank's Staff Training College, Arijit blends experience, academic rigor, and a deep commitment to mentorship.

• • •

Interviewer: "Good morning, Mr. Arijit Dasgupta. First of all, congratulations on being shortlisted for the Scale 4 promotion interview. How are you feeling about it?"

Arijit: "Good morning, Sir. Thank you so much. I feel both excited and slightly nervous. But I'm confident and looking forward to this opportunity."

Interviewer: "That's great to hear, Arijit. I see here that you've been awarded the 'Best Branch Manager' title three times in your career. Quite

an achievement. What drives you to maintain such a high standard of performance year after year?"
(Note: Keep a note of all your achievements and recognitions before you face your promotion interview)

Arijit: "Thank you, Sir. I believe my passion for problem-solving is a key factor that drives me to maintain high performance. I genuinely enjoy identifying challenges, whether they pertain to customer satisfaction, branch profitability, or staff motivation, and working towards innovative solutions that create value for everyone involved. Another significant aspect is the strong connection I share with my team. I have always believed in empowering my staff, creating an open environment where they feel motivated and heard. A cohesive team can achieve far more than an individual, and I make it a point to align everyone with common goals while also recognizing their individual contributions.

Moreover, the trust and faith my customers place in me and my branch inspire me every day. When a customer walks in with a problem or a financial need and walks out satisfied, it's a powerful reminder of the impact we, as bankers, have on people's lives. Each branch I've managed has posed unique challenges, whether it was navigating the complexities of rural banking in Gaya or addressing the high-volume demands in Tinsukia. Overcoming these challenges through meticulous planning, collaboration, and customer-centric strategies has been immensely rewarding.

Lastly, I believe in continuous learning and adaptability. Banking is an evolving field, and staying updated on regulations, technologies, and best practices has helped me consistently perform at a high standard. These elements together create a cycle of motivation that keeps me striving for excellence, year after year."

Interviewer: "Speaking of challenges, I understand you've worked in rural areas like Gaya and semi-urban areas like Tinsukia. Can you tell me about one particularly troublesome loan case you've handled and how you managed it?"

Arijit: "Certainly, Sir. During my tenure in Gaya, we had a farmer who had availed a term loan for purchasing a tractor. Due to consecutive poor harvests, he defaulted on multiple EMIs, and the account turned into an NPA. The situation escalated when he refused to cooperate in restructuring the loan. I worked with my team to initiate discussions with the local Panchayat. By involving influential village leaders and creating a repayment plan aligned with his crop cycles, we managed to regularize the account within six months. It was a challenging yet satisfying experience."

Interviewer: "That's a commendable approach, Arijit. Now, let's shift to Letters of Credit. Can you explain the difference between Red Clause LC and Green Clause LC?"

Arijit: "Certainly, Sir. A Red Clause LC provides pre-shipment advances to the exporter, enabling them to prepare goods for shipment. It is backed by the issuing bank, which bears the risk. On the other hand, a Green Clause LC extends this facility by also covering storage and logistics expenses at the port. This added feature provides exporters with greater financial flexibility."

Interviewer: "That's absolutely correct. Moving forward, let's talk about Debt Service Coverage Ratio (DSCR). What thresholds must a borrower meet for Net DSCR and Gross DSCR?"

Arijit: "Sir, the Net DSCR, which excludes interest payable, must be above 2. The Gross DSCR, including interest payable, should not fall below 1.75. These thresholds ensure the borrower's capacity to service their debt obligations."

Interviewer: "Excellent. Now, since housing loans are critical to retail banking, what precautions do you take during the disbursement of such loans?"

Arijit: "Sir, I follow a meticulous process. First, I ensure the disbursement aligns with the construction stages if it's not an outright purchase. I verify inspection records to track progress post-sanction. Additionally, I insist on proof of material purchases before releasing advance payments. For builder payments, I ensure they're made directly via RTGS or NEFT and supported by a Letter of Authority from the borrower. I also verify the sale deed amount against the agreement to avoid discrepancies. Lastly, I ensure the borrower contributes their margin proportionally before each disbursement."

Interviewer: "That's a comprehensive answer, Arijit. Now let's consider a more challenging hypothetical scenario. A cyber-attack disrupts the bank's operations, affecting online banking services and ATM networks. Customers are panicking, and social media is flooded with complaints. Outline the steps you would take to manage the crisis, restore services, and communicate effectively with stakeholders."

Arijit: "Sir, a cyber-attack demands immediate containment and clear communication. My first step would be to activate the bank's Cyber Incident Response Plan, involving the IT security team to isolate affected systems and collaborate with experts to identify the breach's scope. Containment minimizes further damage while the team works on restoring services.

Simultaneously, transparent communication with customers and stakeholders is crucial. I would issue updates via SMS, email, and social media, assuring customers their funds and data are secure while providing realistic service restoration timelines. Setting up a dedicated helpline and deploying staff to handle queries empathetically would reduce panic.

Operationally, I'd ensure branches maintain adequate cash reserves to support offline or manual withdrawals, reconciling them later. Staff would be briefed to provide consistent, accurate information and prioritize urgent customer needs.

I'd also escalate the matter to senior management and regulatory authorities like the RBI to align our response with industry protocols. Post-restoration, I'd work with IT to enhance cybersecurity measures, such as system updates and employee awareness training, to prevent recurrence.

Balancing swift technical resolution with customer-centric communication and regulatory compliance ensures crisis management is effective and instills trust in the bank."

Interviewer: "Well thought out. Before we wrap up, let's touch upon your personal aspirations. You mentioned you're pursuing a PhD in Management. How do you see this contributing to your career in banking?"

Arijit: "Sir, my PhD focuses on leadership strategies in the banking sector. It's not just about academic pursuit; it's a step toward my goal of becoming an instructor at the bank's staff training college. I want to leverage my experience and knowledge to mentor the next generation of bankers."

Interviewer: "That's a noble goal, Arijit. Before we proceed further, I noticed you have a keen interest in retail products. Can you briefly tell me your thoughts on reverse mortgage loans and their relevance in India?"

Arijit: "Certainly, Sir. Reverse mortgage loans provide senior citizens with an additional income source by leveraging their self-occupied property. In India, where retirement planning is often inadequate, this product offers financial independence to retirees. However, its adoption is limited due to cultural factors like the reluctance to mortgage ancestral properties."

Interviewer: "Arijit, let's move to another important area of banking. You are tasked with leading a financial literacy campaign in a remote rural area. The villagers are hesitant to open bank accounts due to trust issues and lack of awareness. What steps would you take to promote financial inclusion and build trust with the community?"

Arijit: "Sir, promoting financial inclusion in rural areas requires a personalized and community-oriented approach. I would begin by conducting village-level meetings, involving local leaders like sarpanches and school teachers, who are trusted by the community. Simplifying banking concepts in the local language and using relatable examples to explain the benefits of savings accounts, insurance, and digital payments would help bridge the knowledge gap.

To build trust, I'd focus on demonstrating transparency and reliability. For example, facilitating door-to-door services for account opening and ensuring a hassle-free process with minimal documentation would encourage participation. I would also organize workshops to educate villagers about government schemes like PMJDY and ensure they understand how these initiatives benefit them directly.

Additionally, setting up temporary kiosks or camps for on-the-spot account opening and small financial transactions would reinforce the accessibility of banking services. Engaging local influencers and sharing success stories from neighboring villages would further build credibility and trust within the community."

Interviewer: "That's a thoughtful approach. Let's tackle a different challenge. A market shock causes a steep decline in the value of government securities held in the bank's portfolio, impacting the bank's profitability. How would you mitigate this market risk and rebalance the portfolio to ensure compliance with SLR requirements?"

Arijit: "Sir, managing market risk during such a shock requires immediate action and a long-term strategy. I would first assess the impact on the bank's profitability and SLR compliance. To manage the shortfall, I'd prioritize liquidating non-core assets or low-yield investments to maintain liquidity and meet the SLR requirements.

Simultaneously, I would work with the treasury team to hedge against further declines using instruments like interest rate swaps or forward rate agreements, aligning with RBI regulations. Rebalancing the portfolio would involve shifting a portion of the holdings to shorter-duration securities, which are less sensitive to interest rate fluctuations, while gradually rebuilding exposure to higher-yield securities when the market stabilizes.

On a broader level, I would collaborate with risk management teams to enhance stress-testing mechanisms, ensuring the portfolio is better equipped to handle future shocks. Regular reviews and diversification of the investment portfolio would be integral to mitigating such risks."

Interviewer: "Excellent. Now, here's a scenario involving corporate banking. A corporate client has unhedged foreign exchange exposure, and you anticipate significant currency volatility. How would you guide the client to mitigate their forex risk while ensuring compliance with RBI regulations?"

Arijit: "Sir, managing forex risk for a corporate client begins with educating them about the potential implications of currency volatility on their financials. I would recommend entering into hedging instruments like forward contracts, currency options, or swaps, depending on their exposure and risk appetite. For example, a forward contract would lock in an exchange rate for future payments, providing certainty amid volatility.

To ensure compliance with RBI regulations, I'd guide them to document the underlying exposure for the hedging transaction, ensuring the instrument aligns with their genuine business requirements. It's also crucial to avoid speculative transactions, focusing solely on risk mitigation.

Additionally, I'd encourage the client to regularly review their forex positions and integrate forex risk management into their overall financial strategy. Providing regular updates on market trends and engaging them in scenario analysis would help them make informed decisions."

Interviewer: "Arijit, your answers today have been comprehensive, thoughtful, and reflective of a deep understanding of banking operations. It's clear that your experience and continuous learning have shaped you into a well-rounded professional. I wish you all the best for this promotion and hope to see you excel as a Chief Manager soon."

Arijit: "Thank you so much, Sir. It has been an honor to interact with you. I truly appreciate your insights and encouragement, and I look forward to contributing even more effectively to the bank in the future."

Interviewer: "Best of luck, Arijit. Keep striving for excellence!"

• • •

CHAPTER XVII

Leading with Empathy and Execution: Anjali Nair's Rise to Officer Cadre

Interview Snapshot - (Senior Clerk to Scale I)
This interview with Anjali Nair is a playbook on modern-day leadership, empathy, and precision in banking. From navigating cyberattacks and politically sensitive NPAs to balancing single motherhood and professional ambition, her responses offer practical insights, emotional intelligence, and operational sharpness. She doesn't just answer questions—she solves problems. Whether it's streamlining queue times or salvaging customer trust after compliance challenges, Anjali shows how resilience, adaptability, and strategy can coexist. This one is not just worth reading—it's worth studying.

Candidate Profile - Anjali Nair (Senior Clerk)
Anjali Nair, a Senior Clerk at Indian Overseas Bank, is currently posted in Vijayawada, Andhra Pradesh, with a decade of dedicated service. A CAIIB distinction holder, she has consistently demonstrated innovation and impact—most notably by reducing cash counter queue times by 30% and leading a financial literacy campaign that reached over 2,000 rural households. Her efforts earned her recognition in a regional newspaper. Despite the challenges of being a single mother to two young children, Anjali remains driven by purpose and resilience, aspiring to grow professionally while continuing to make a difference in the communities she serves.

• • •

Interviewer: "Good morning, Ms. Anjali. Welcome back! It's great to see you progressing further in the promotion process. How are you feeling today?"

    Anjali: "Good morning, Sir. Thank you for having me. I'm a bit nervous but excited about this opportunity."

    Interviewer: *[Smiling]* "Nervousness is a sign that you care, and that's always a good start. Let's dive straight into it. Anjali, as someone who has spent a decade in banking and achieved remarkable milestones, what do you believe is the single most underrated skill for a banker, and why?"

Anjali: "Sir, adaptability. The banking industry evolves rapidly with technological advancements, regulatory changes, and shifting customer expectations. A banker who can adapt quickly not only stays relevant but also thrives under changing circumstances. It's a skill I prioritize, especially given the dynamic nature of my roles."

Interviewer:[*Leaning forward*] "Interesting perspective. Now, let's address a potential challenge. Suppose you're promoted to branch manager, and within the first month, your branch faces a cyberattack where customer data is compromised. How would you handle this situation to safeguard the bank's reputation?"

Anjali: [*Pauses thoughtfully*] "Sir, the first step would be immediate containment. I'd notify the bank's cybersecurity team and ensure systems are isolated to prevent further breaches. Simultaneously, I'd inform customers, maintaining complete transparency, and provide guidance on securing their accounts. Internally, I'd ensure the team is trained to handle customer queries empathetically. Post-incident, I'd collaborate with senior management to strengthen systems and rebuild customer trust through proactive communication and outreach programs."

Interviewer:[*Nods approvingly*] "Crisis management under pressure; very well articulated. Now let's pivot to something more reflective. You've balanced a demanding career and personal life admirably. What's a lesson from your personal struggles that you've applied successfully in your professional journey?"

Anjali: [*Smiling*] "Resilience, Sir. When life throws change, you adapt and move forward. In banking, there are days when everything goes wrong – systems fail, customers are irate, targets feel impossible. I've learned to focus on solutions rather than problems and to inspire the same mindset in my team."

Interviewer:[*Leaning back*] "Resilience and leadership – that's a strong combination. Let's come to your notable achievement which you have written in the achievements section of your promotion form i.e. reducing cash counter queues by 30%. If you were asked to replicate this success for an underperforming urban branch, but with a significantly larger customer base and a reluctant team, how would you approach it?"

Anjali: [*Confidently*] "Sir, I'd begin with a thorough branch audit to identify pain points specific to the location, such as process bottlenecks or technology gaps. I'd involve the team early on, addressing their reluctance by demonstrating the tangible benefits of the changes. Customized training sessions and incentives for staff could boost participation. For customers, I'd use targeted outreach to promote digital banking solutions and consider piloting initiatives like extended banking hours or self-service kiosks."

Interviewer:[*Raising an eyebrow*] "A strategic and inclusive approach. Now let's talk about nonperforming assets. Imagine you're tasked with recovering a large NPA from a politically connected borrower in a small town. Local authorities are uncooperative, and the borrower has influence over the community. What's your strategy?"

Anjali: [*Pauses briefly*] "Sir, this requires a tactful balance of assertiveness and diplomacy. First, I'd ensure our legal documentation is airtight and leverage available legal tools like SARFAESI. I'd also approach higher authorities within the bank to engage senior officials who can mediate with local authorities. Parallelly, I'd explore alternative resolutions, such as restructuring the loan if the borrower shows willingness. Maintaining transparency and ensuring the community sees the bank's actions as fair is crucial to avoid backlash."

Interviewer:[*Grinning slightly*] "And what if the borrower refuses to negotiate and rallies public sentiment against the bank?"

Anjali: [*Firmer tone*] "In that case, Sir, I'd escalate to the district administration and the police, ensuring the situation doesn't spiral into law-and-order issues. Meanwhile, I'd organize community meetings to communicate the bank's perspective and highlight the importance of recovery for broader economic benefits. Persistence and clear communication are key."

Interviewer:[*Leaning in*] "Impressive adaptability under pressure. Now, let's discuss a broader issue. Why do you think digital transformation in banking is often met with resistance, and how can leaders overcome it?"

Anjali: "Sir, resistance to digital transformation stems from fear of change, lack of skills, and concerns about job security. Leaders can address this by creating a culture of learning and innovation. Regular training programs, involving employees in decision-making, and demonstrating how technology complements rather than replaces human roles can ease the transition. Recognizing and rewarding early adopters also creates a ripple effect of acceptance."

Interviewer: "That's heartwarming and aligns perfectly with the mission of banking inclusivity. Now, let's take a hypothetical scenario. Suppose a major MSME client with an overdraft account has been consistently exceeding their limit without prior approval. Despite repeated warnings, the customer continues this practice, citing temporary cash flow issues. How would you address this situation while maintaining the client relationship?"

Anjali: *[Thoughtfully]* "Sir, handling such a situation requires a balance between enforcing discipline and supporting the client's business. First, I'd arrange a meeting with the client to understand their cash flow challenges in detail. Based on the insights, I'd evaluate whether their overdraft limit needs to be reassessed and possibly increased, provided their business fundamentals remain strong. At the same time, I'd establish stricter monitoring mechanisms, such as setting alerts for limit breaches and periodic reviews. Educating the client on the risks of consistent overuse and advising them on alternative financing options, such as working capital loans, could also help. Sir, this approach demonstrates empathy while ensuring the bank's interests are safeguarded."

Interviewer: *[Switching gears]* "Fair point. Now, let's test your financial knowledge. Why are capital adequacy ratios critical for banks, and how do they impact lending policies?"

Anjali: "Sir, capital adequacy ratios ensure that banks have sufficient capital to absorb losses, protecting depositors and maintaining financial stability. A higher ratio allows more room for lending, while a lower ratio restricts it. These ratios also influence a bank's risk appetite and are key metrics for regulatory compliance."

Interviewer: " Anjali, let's look into the future. How do you see Indian banking evolving in the next decade, and where do you see yourself contributing?"

Anjali: *[Confidently]* "Sir, Indian banking is moving towards greater digitization, financial inclusion, and sustainable financing. The focus will increasingly be on personalized services and ESG-linked products. I envision myself leading a branch or a regional office that sets benchmarks in innovation and customer satisfaction, while also mentoring future bankers to thrive in this evolving landscape."

Interviewer: "You're doing well, Anjali. Let's move on to a situation that tests your customer relationship management skills. Suppose a high-net-worth individual (HNI) customer complains about repeated errors in their account statements and threatens to move all their accounts to another bank. How would you resolve the issue, ensure it does not recur, and retain the customer?"

Anjali: *[Calm and confident]* "Sir, I'd first meet the customer in person or have a detailed conversation to apologize for the inconvenience and assure them that their concerns are being taken seriously. Immediate steps would involve rectifying the errors in their account statements and providing a clear explanation of how they occurred. To prevent recurrence, I'd initiate an internal audit of the processes responsible for these errors and implement corrective measures, such as additional checks or system upgrades. Lastly, I'd offer personalized service, such as assigning a relationship manager to handle their account and introducing exclusive benefits to rebuild trust and reinforce their value to our bank."

Interviewer: *[Nods approvingly]* "Proactive and empathetic approach, well done. Now, let's address a leadership scenario. One of your branch officers has been underperforming and consistently failing to meet targets. Despite providing training and support, there has been no improvement. How would you address this issue, ensuring the staff member gets a fair chance while maintaining branch performance?"

Anjali: *[Firmly]* "Sir, I'd begin by revisiting their performance through one-on-one discussions to identify any overlooked factors—personal issues, misaligned role expectations, or skill gaps. If the issue persists, I'd consider reshuffling their responsibilities to a role better suited to their strengths while setting clear, achievable goals. Concurrently, I'd reassign some responsibilities to other team members temporarily to maintain branch performance. If there's still no improvement after giving them every opportunity, I'd escalate the matter for further action per Officers Service Regulations Act and also our bank's HR protocols. Throughout, I'd ensure the staff member feels supported and treated fairly."

Interviewer: *[Raising an eyebrow]* "Balanced and professional. Now, let's tackle a delicate compliance question. A new customer with a large deposit potential approaches your branch but has a history of being flagged for suspicious transactions in another bank. How would you assess and onboard the customer while adhering to KYC/AML guidelines?"

Anjali:*[Carefully]* "Sir, I'd follow a stringent due diligence process. First, I'd ensure the customer completes our KYC requirements, verifying all documents thoroughly. I'd use additional tools like CIBIL checks and information from FIU-IND to gather insights into their financial behavior. If the flagged transactions in the other bank indicate potential money laundering or fraudulent activities, I'd seek further clarification from the customer and escalate the case to our compliance team for a detailed review. Only if the compliance team clears the account would I proceed with onboarding, while setting transaction monitoring alerts to ensure continued vigilance."

Interviewer:*[Leaning back]* "Impressive, Anjali. You've shown clarity and maturity in handling complex scenarios. As we conclude, I must say, your ability to balance customer satisfaction, compliance, and team management is commendable. Do you have any questions for us?"

Anjali:*[Smiling]* "Thank you, Sir. I'd just like to understand how the bank envisions utilizing its middle management for driving digital transformation initiatives at the branch level. It's an area I'm deeply interested in contributing to."

Interviewer: *[Smiling warmly]* "That's a thoughtful question. Digital transformation indeed requires middle managers to bridge the gap between strategy and execution. I'm glad to see your interest in it. Anjali, you've presented yourself exceptionally today. All the best for the next steps, and thank you for your time.

• • •

CHAPTER XVIII

From Viral Complaints to ₹500 Crore Loans: Inside Jaskeerat Kaur's Thrilling Promotion Interview Journey

Interview Snapshot - (Scale II to III)

This gripping interview with Jaskeerat Kaur is a masterclass in handling high-stakes banking with grace and precision. From managing ₹500 crore credit decisions to defusing viral social media complaints, she navigates every challenge with a sharp risk mindset and genuine leadership. Her answers blend technical depth with emotional intelligence—covering neobanks, CDS, market risk, and team management in real-world settings. Whether you're preparing for complex credit questions or crisis response, this interview gives you the mindset and language of a true future-ready leader.

Candidate Profile - Jaskeerat Kaur (Credit Manager, Scale II)

Jaskeerat Kaur, a dedicated Credit Officer (Scale 2) at Punjab & Sind Bank, brings 8 years of focused banking experience with a specialization in credit and risk management. A certified professional by IIBF, she has led high-stakes assignments—including the bank's largest corporate loan sanction of ₹500 crore. Her innovative credit risk evaluation model, now adopted bank-wide, earned her recognition in the bank's internal newsletter. Despite the recent personal loss of her father, Jaskeerat continues to excel professionally while serving as the primary caregiver for her younger siblings, embodying resilience, leadership, and unwavering commitment under pressure.

• • •

Interviewer: "Good morning, Ms. Jaskeerat Kaur. First of all, congratulations on making it this far in your promotion journey. It's a pleasure to meet someone with such a decorated profile. Eight years as a Credit Officer and a remarkable record like yours... that's quite impressive."

Jaskeerat: "Thank you, Sir. It's an honor to be here today. I'm looking forward to this opportunity to grow further in my banking career."

Interviewer: "Before we dive into the technical aspects, let me ask you something personal, Jaskeerat. I noticed you've taken on a lot of responsibilities outside of work recently, being the primary caregiver for your siblings after the loss of your father. How have you managed to balance these personal challenges with your professional commitments?"

Jaskeerat:*[Pausing briefly, visibly moved but composed]* "Thank you for asking, Sir. It hasn't been easy, but I believe the support of my family and colleagues has been my biggest strength. At work, I focus on planning and prioritizing, while at home, I try to be a role model for my siblings. I've also taken inspiration from my father's values, which keep me motivated."

Interviewer: *[Nodding empathetically]* "That's admirable, Jaskeerat. Now, let's pivot to your professional experience. You've been a Credit Officer for eight years and even led the sanctioning of a   ₹500-crore corporate loan. Tell me, what's the biggest challenge you faced during that process, and how did you overcome it?"

Jaskeerat: "Sir, the biggest challenge was ensuring the creditworthiness of the borrower given the size of the loan. It required extensive due diligence, including assessing financials, projections, and market conditions. I had to coordinate with multiple departments to ensure all risks were identified and mitigated. We introduced a customized credit risk assessment model, which provided a clear risk rating. Additionally, I ensured frequent discussions with the client's management to build mutual trust and transparency."

Interviewer: "Impressive. Speaking of risk, let's move to a hypothetical scenario. Suppose you are the Branch Manager of a semi-urban branch, and a large SME client suddenly defaults on a significant loan, impacting your branch's NPA ratio. How would you address this situation to minimize damage?"

Jaskeerat: "Sir, in such a scenario, my immediate step would be to analyze the root cause of the default. If the reason is temporary cash flow issues, I would suggest restructuring the loan or offering a moratorium period. Simultaneously, I'd initiate recovery proceedings under SARFAESI or other applicable frameworks if the borrower shows no intent to repay. Additionally, I would explore alternate revenue streams and recovery efforts to stabilize the branch's financials while regularly updating higher management."

Interviewer: *[Smiling]* "That's a well-thought-out approach. Let's switch gears now. Neobanks are becoming a buzzword in the industry. Can you explain what a neobank is and how our bank can counter the competition posed by them?"

Jaskeerat: "Certainly, Sir. A neobank is a fully digital bank that operates without physical branches. They leverage technology to provide seamless and customer-centric services. To counter them, our bank could focus on improving its digital offerings, such as mobile banking apps and customer service chatbots. Additionally, promoting hybrid banking—combining digital convenience with physical branch support—could give us a competitive edge. Strengthening data analytics for personalized offerings and ensuring robust cybersecurity would also be key."

Interviewer: *[Leaning forward slightly]* "Good point. Moving on, can you explain the '4-eyes principle' and why it's critical in banking?"

Jaskeerat: "Yes, Sir. The '4-eyes principle' mandates that critical banking tasks require dual authorization or review by two individuals. For example, loan sanctions, high-value transactions, and reconciliations must involve at least two officials. This ensures better control, reduces the risk of fraud, and upholds compliance."

Interviewer: *[Smiling]* "You've explained that well. Now, let's discuss a recent regulatory change. Are you aware of the new nomination rules for deposit accounts? Could you elaborate on them?"

Jaskeerat: "Certainly, Sir. The new rules now allow up to four nominees for a deposit account, which wasn't the case earlier. Depositors can choose between two types of nominations: successive or simultaneous. In successive nominations, a priority order is defined, such as first, second, third, and fourth nominees. At any point, only the nominee highest in the order will be effective. In simultaneous nomination, the share of each nominee is predetermined. This change enhances flexibility for account holders."

Interviewer: "Excellent. Now, let's talk about financial instruments. Could you explain what a Credit Default Swap (CDS) is and its significance in banking?"

Jaskeerat: "Of course, Sir. A CDS is a financial derivative that acts as insurance against the default of a borrower. The buyer of a CDS pays a premium to the seller in exchange for compensation if the borrower defaults. For banks, CDS can mitigate credit risk, allowing them to transfer risk exposure to other entities, thus maintaining financial stability."

Interviewer: *[Raising an eyebrow]* "That's accurate. Let me test your understanding of market risk in banking. What are the key types of market risk, and how do banks manage them?"

Jaskeerat: "Market risk in banking arises from fluctuations in interest rates, exchange rates, and asset prices. The main types are interest rate risk, foreign exchange risk, and equity risk. Banks manage market risk using hedging instruments like derivatives, asset-liability matching, and Value at Risk (VaR) models. Robust monitoring frameworks and stress testing are also integral to identifying and mitigating these risks."

Interviewer: *[Leaning back in his chair]* "Well done, Jaskeerat. Now, here's a tricky one. Imagine a situation where you suspect a subordinate of bypassing the 4-eyes principle to process unauthorized transactions. How would you handle it?"

Jaskeerat: "Sir, I'd first gather evidence by reviewing the transactions in question and analyzing logs or approvals. Once I have substantial proof, I'd discreetly confront the subordinate and give them an opportunity to explain. If the violation is confirmed, I will escalate the matter to HR or higher management, ensuring a thorough investigation while maintaining confidentiality."

Interviewer: *[Smiling broadly]* "That's a thoughtful and balanced response. Jaskeerat, with your experience and expertise, where do you see yourself contributing the most value if promoted to Scale 3?"

Jaskeerat: *[Smiling confidently]* "Sir, as a Scale 3 officer, I envision myself taking on a leadership role in credit risk management, mentoring junior staff, and driving innovative solutions. My goal would be to enhance portfolio quality, ensure compliance, and contribute to the bank's profitability by leveraging my experience and skills."

Interviewer: "Jaskeerat, before we wrap up, I'd like to pose a few more challenging scenarios to get a sense of your problem-solving and leadership abilities. Imagine your branch has been chosen to pilot a new work structure requiring staff to multitask across roles. While this aims to improve efficiency, it has faced resistance from staff who fear job insecurity. How would you implement the change and address these concerns?"

Jaskeerat: "Sir, change is always challenging, especially when it impacts employees directly. My first step would be transparent communication. I'd organize a meeting with the staff to explain the rationale behind the new work structure, emphasizing how it is intended to enhance operational efficiency rather than threaten job security. I'd also highlight how learning new skills could improve their career prospects. Next, I'd implement the change gradually, starting with volunteers to build trust. Regular training sessions would be arranged to equip staff for the new roles. Lastly, I'd establish an open feedback loop where employees can voice concerns and provide suggestions, making them feel heard and valued."

Interviewer: "Good approach, Jaskeerat. Change management is as much about empathy as it is about execution. Now, consider this situation: A borrower seeks to foreclose their loan but disputes the amount due, claiming errors in interest calculations. Your team's review finds no errors, but the customer remains adamant. How would you handle this dispute to avoid escalation and ensure customer satisfaction?"

Jaskeerat: "Sir, in such situations, maintaining professionalism and building trust is key. I'd first ensure the borrower feels heard by listening to their concerns patiently. Next, I'd arrange a one-on-one meeting to explain the interest calculations in detail, using transparent documentation to back up the findings. If necessary, I'd involve the audit team or a third party for an independent review to assure the customer of impartiality. To further reassure them, I'd propose flexible options like adjusting minor discrepancies or offering a goodwill gesture, provided it aligns with the bank's policies. The focus would be on resolving the issue amicably and retaining the customer's trust."

Interviewer:[*Smiling slightly*] "That's a practical and customer-focused approach. Now for the final scenario. Imagine a customer posts a viral negative review about your branch's services on social media, alleging poor handling of their issue. The review contains the account number as well. The regional office asks for an immediate resolution and response. How would you manage the situation to protect the bank's reputation?"

Jaskeerat: "Sir, in such a sensitive situation, time is of the essence. I'd first contact the customer directly to understand their grievances and resolve the issue to their satisfaction. A personalized apology, combined with swift corrective action, can go a long way in defusing the situation. Concurrently, I'd prepare a formal response for social media, acknowledging the issue without admitting fault prematurely, and assure the public that the matter is being addressed. Once resolved, I'd request the customer to update their post about the positive resolution. Additionally, I'd coordinate with the regional office to implement measures to prevent such incidents in the future."

Interviewer: [*Leaning back, smiling warmly*] "Jaskeerat, I must say your answers reflect not just your technical knowledge but also your leadership and emotional intelligence. It's evident you're prepared to handle the multifaceted challenges of a higher role. Before we conclude, let me ask you this: what drives you to excel in banking, and where do you see yourself contributing the most as you progress in your career?"

Jaskeerat:[*Smiling confidently*] "Thank you, Sir. What drives me is the sense of purpose banking provides in shaping communities and supporting economic growth. I find great fulfillment in helping businesses and individuals achieve their goals. In the long term, I see myself contributing by leading strategic initiatives in credit risk management, mentoring the next generation of bankers, and ensuring sustainable growth for the bank."

Interviewer: [*Standing up and extending a hand*] "Thank you, Jaskeerat. It's been a pleasure talking to you. Your responses were insightful and inspiring, and I wish you all the best for the next steps in this process. If there's one thing I've learned today, it's that you're not just a capable banker but also a compassionate leader."

Jaskeerat:[*Standing and shaking hands*] "Thank you so much, Sir. This interview has been a great learning experience, and I appreciate the opportunity to present my views. I look forward to contributing more to the bank's success."

• • •

CHAPTER XIX

When Rural Grit Meets Urban Ambition: The Interview That Tested More Than Banking Skills

Interview Snapshot - (Scale I to II)
What happens when a banker shaped by the sands of Barmer is tested on urban complexities, treasury concepts, and moral leadership—all in one interview? Dinesh Choudhary's mock interview is a deep dive into the mind of a rural champion navigating ethical dilemmas, CRR policy shifts, fraudulent practices, and forex fluctuations. His honest answers and calm crisis handling reflect more than textbook knowledge—they reveal emotional intelligence, commitment, and sharp judgment. A compelling read for anyone aiming to blend values with vision in a high-pressure interview room.

Candidate Profile - Dinesh Choudhary (Assistant Manager, Scale 1)
Dinesh Choudhary, currently posted as an Assistant Manager (Scale 1) in Barmer, Rajasthan, brings six years of hands-on banking experience, with a strong focus on rural credit, microfinance, and financial inclusion. Originally from Jodhpur, he has spent the past four years navigating the challenges of banking in desert terrain, working tirelessly to deliver priority sector lending and digital banking solutions to underserved communities. His certifications in JAIIB, Treasury Management, and Microfinance reflect his technical foundation and commitment to continued learning.

Dinesh has disbursed over ₹50 crore in PSL loans with minimal delinquency and has played a vital role in empowering women-led SHGs and small-scale farmers through micro-loans and financial awareness campaigns. His treasury knowledge, though limited to regional forex dealings, has proven useful in facilitating trade for local importers.

Amid these professional achievements, Dinesh faces a deeply personal challenge—his wife suffers from a chronic illness requiring regular care in Jodhpur. Balancing work commitments in Barmer with limited opportunities to be by her side causes emotional strain. Still, his dedication to his role remains unwavering.

Aspiring for a Scale 2 role in an urban center, Dinesh hopes to broaden his banking exposure while achieving better work-life balance. His resilience, empathy, and rural expertise position him strongly for elevation.

• • •

Interviewer: Good morning, Mr. Dinesh Choudhary. Welcome. How are you feeling today?

Dinesh Choudhary: Good morning, sir. I'm feeling positive and prepared, though I must admit there's always a hint of nervous energy in such settings.

Interviewer: *[Smiling]* "That's natural. A little nervousness keeps us sharp. Let's begin. Could you briefly walk me through your journey in banking so far?"

Dinesh: "Certainly, sir. I started my career as a clerk and, through consistent performance and dedication, rose to the position of Assistant Manager in Scale 1. I've spent the last four years in Barmer, Rajasthan—a region with its unique challenges—managing rural credit disbursement, microfinance, and leading financial literacy campaigns, especially targeting women-led SHGs and small-scale farmers. My work in Priority Sector Lending has allowed me to disburse over ₹50 crore with minimal defaults. Additionally, I've conducted over 30 financial awareness camps and handled forex transactions for local traders."

Interviewer: "That's impressive. Now, on a personal note—balancing professional excellence with personal challenges requires resilience. As I can read from your promotion form regarding your wife's health. Given your wife's health concerns and the distance from Jodhpur, how have you managed to maintain focus at work?"

Dinesh: *[Pausing thoughtfully]* "It's been difficult, sir. My wife's health is a constant concern, and being away adds to the emotional strain. However, my commitment to serving rural communities has been my anchor. The trust people place in us as bankers drives me to give my best. I also find that staying engaged with meaningful work helps me manage personal stress better."

Interviewer: "That's commendable. It speaks volumes about your mental strength. Now, let's pivot to your work experience. You've excelled in rural credit disbursement. Tell me about a time when you faced a major challenge in disbursing credit in Barmer. How did you handle it?"

Dinesh: "One instance that stands out was during a severe drought in Barmer. Many small farmers were in urgent need of credit, but their repayment capacity was questionable. Balancing risk assessment with the need for financial inclusion was critical. I collaborated with local self-help groups, used alternative credit appraisal methods like community-based assessments, and structured repayment schedules aligned with their crop cycles. This approach minimized defaults and ensured timely credit disbursement."

Interviewer: *[Leaning forward]* "Interesting. Let's test your decision-making in a hypothetical scenario. Imagine you're now in an urban branch handling a large corporate loan. A client requests an urgent sanction, but the collateral documents seem incomplete, though from a reputed company. What would you do?"

Dinesh: "Regardless of the client's reputation, due diligence cannot be compromised. I would prioritize verifying the documents, escalate the issue to the appropriate credit risk team if needed, and request temporary clarifications. If it's a matter of urgency, I might suggest structuring the sanction in phases—approving the portion that's secure while holding back the rest until full compliance."

Interviewer:*[Nods, then suddenly shifts gears]* "Good. Now, tell me—what would happen to the Indian banking system if the CRR (Cash Reserve Ratio) is reduced by 1% overnight?"

Dinesh:*[Responds swiftly]* "A reduction in the CRR by 1% would release more funds into the banking system, increasing liquidity. This could lower interest rates as banks have more funds to lend, potentially boosting credit growth. However, if not managed carefully, it might also lead to inflationary pressures due to increased money supply."

Interviewer: "Sharp answer. Moving to your certifications—since you're a Certified Treasury Professional, explain the difference between an interest rate swap and a currency swap."

Dinesh: "An interest rate swap is an agreement between two parties to exchange interest payments on a notional principal, typically swapping fixed rates with floating rates to manage interest rate risk. A currency swap, on the other hand, involves exchanging principal and interest payments in different currencies, helping manage foreign exchange risk along with interest rate fluctuations."

Interviewer:[*Raises an eyebrow*] "Speaking of foreign exchange, how would an unexpected depreciation of the Indian Rupee impact the rural economy in Barmer?"

Dinesh: "A depreciation of the rupee could have mixed effects. For local traders involved in exporting goods, it might be beneficial as their products become cheaper in foreign markets. However, for importers in Barmer, especially those dealing with Middle Eastern goods, costs would rise. Additionally, inflationary pressures due to costlier imports could increase the cost of agricultural inputs, indirectly affecting farmers."

Interviewer:[*Smiling, sensing Dinesh's comfort*] "Excellent. Now, let's add a twist. Imagine you're leading a team, and one of your subordinates is manipulating microfinance records to meet disbursement targets. You discover this during an internal audit. What would you do?"

Dinesh: [*Firmly*] "That's a serious breach of ethics and compliance. I would first gather all the facts to ensure there's no misunderstanding. If confirmed, I'd report it to the compliance and HR departments as per protocol. Simultaneously, I'd initiate corrective measures to address any financial discrepancies caused. Transparency is non-negotiable in such cases."

Interviewer: [*Pauses, then throws a bouncer*] "Final question, Dinesh. You've mentioned your aspirations for an urban posting. But what if I tell you that your promotion comes with another rural posting, even more remote than Barmer? Would you accept it?"

Dinesh: [*After a brief pause*] "Sir, while I've personal reasons for seeking an urban posting, my professional commitment remains to the organization. If the role demands me to serve in a remote area, I will fulfill that duty with the same dedication I've shown in Barmer. However, I would also request consideration for a future urban posting, balancing both professional growth and personal circumstances."

Interviewer:[*Resuming with a Focused Tone*] "Dinesh, you've demonstrated strong practical insights so far. Now, I'll ask you some conceptual questions to assess your foundational knowledge in banking and finance.Which devices are examples of AI applications in banking that are transforming traditional front-desk operations?"

Dinesh: "Chatbots are prime examples of AI-led devices in banking. They offer digitized, customized, and interactive customer experiences, handling queries efficiently while reducing operational costs."

Interviewer: *[Leaning forward with a quick shift]* "In the context of international finance, what does the term "export" encompass under regulatory frameworks?"

Dinesh: "Export refers to both the physical movement of goods from India to a place outside India and the provision of services from India to any person located outside the country. This comprehensive definition ensures all cross-border commercial activities are covered under export finance regulations."

Interviewer: *[Raises an eyebrow, adding complexity]* "When assessing working capital, what is meant by the "working capital gap," and why is it significant?"

Dinesh: "The working capital gap represents the difference between current assets and current liabilities, excluding bank borrowings. It indicates the actual shortfall in working capital that needs to be financed, helping banks determine the borrower's funding requirements effectively."

Interviewer: *[Pausing briefly, then concluding with a challenging question]* "Let's discuss mortgages. Which type of mortgage do bankers generally avoid due to the absence of a personal covenant for repayment?"

Dinesh: "Bankers typically avoid usufructuary mortgages because they lack a personal covenant for repayment. In such cases, the lender relies solely on the income generated from the mortgaged property, which increases credit risk."

Interviewer: *[Smiling slightly]* "Thank you, Dinesh. Your responses have been insightful, reflecting both theoretical understanding and practical experience."

Dinesh: *[with confidence]* "Thank you, sir. I appreciate the opportunity to discuss my knowledge and experiences."

· · ·

CHAPTER XX

From Zero Branch Experience to Senior Manager? Smita Gokhale's Bold Response to a Promotion Panel's Toughest Questions!

Interview Snapshot - (Scale II to III)

This interview offers a rare behind-the-scenes look at how a risk specialist defends her promotion readiness despite never handling loans or branch banking. Smita Gokhale's responses blend technical sharpness with strategic thinking—tackling questions on Basel norms, CFA progression, country risk ratings, and value at risk. Her real-life case on preventing a high-value fraud, plus her impressive take on borrower character appraisal, make this a compelling read. It's not just an interview—it's a crash course in risk-informed leadership under pressure.

Candidate Profile: Smita Gokhale, (Scale II Manager , Risk Management)

Smita Gokhale, a Scale II Manager in Risk Management, has spent the last decade building deep expertise in the domain, with seven years stationed at the Head Office in Mumbai. A CFA Level 1 holder with JAIIB and CAIIB credentials, Smita brings analytical rigor and regulatory insight to her role. She is responsible for assessing credit, market, and operational risks across the bank, ensuring compliance with RBI guidelines, Basel III norms, and internal policies. Her contributions include evaluating high-risk sectors, leading risk audits, coordinating with cybersecurity teams, and reinforcing the bank's risk governance framework.

Smita's journey is rooted in resilience. Hailing from rural Maharashtra, she lost her father at a young age and has since been the sole caregiver for her younger siblings. Balancing intense professional demands with personal responsibilities has limited her networking opportunities and slowed her pursuit of further certifications. Despite these challenges, she remains committed to personal growth and excellence.

While her career has been focused entirely on risk functions, she acknowledges limited exposure to customer-facing roles and credit underwriting. Her goal is to become a Chief Risk Officer and is currently working toward the FRM certification. Smita's dedication, integrity, and risk acumen make her a valuable asset to the bank's leadership pipeline.

• • •

Interviewer: "Smita, welcome to the interview. You have built a strong foundation in Risk Management over the past seven years at the Head Office, and your CFA Level 1 certification is a testament to your analytical capabilities. Before we begin, let's acknowledge something unusual about your profile—you have never worked in a branch, yet if promoted, the bank might post you as a Senior Branch Manager in any Semi-Urban or Urban branch. How do you plan to handle this challenge?"
(Those bankers who have no branch experience should prepare well for such questions)

Smita Gokhale: "Thank you, Sir! That's indeed a valid concern, and I understand that as a bank officer, I need to be adaptable. While my expertise lies in risk management, I believe strong fundamentals in banking operations, regulatory policies, and financial products will help me transition into a branch role effectively. Moreover, I am a fast learner. If I were assigned a branch, I would immediately start working closely with experienced staff, understand the customer needs, and focus on credit underwriting, asset-liability management, and customer service.

I would also leverage my risk background to ensure robust internal controls, compliance with RBI norms, and fraud prevention mechanisms at the branch. Additionally, I would seek guidance from senior colleagues and take refresher courses on advances and branch banking to bridge any gaps."

Interviewer: "That's a practical approach. However, given that Scale 3 Branch Managers often deal with high-value loan proposals, how would you compensate for your lack of experience in Loans and Advances when making credit decisions?"
(Bankers without experience in loans and advances should be well-prepared to face this question)

Smita Gokhale: "While I may not have directly worked in loan underwriting, my experience in risk management has given me deep exposure to credit risk assessment. I have analyzed credit portfolios, reviewed high-risk accounts, and evaluated loan exposure across different sectors. I would use this experience to scrutinize credit proposals, assess the risk-return dynamics, and ensure adherence to prudent lending practices.

Furthermore, I would focus on data-driven decision-making, thoroughly review financial statements, and work with my credit team to gain insights into lending patterns. My CFA background also helps in financial modeling and stress testing, which are crucial for assessing loan viability."

Interviewer: "That's a convincing argument. Now, let's talk about your CFA qualification. You cleared Level 1, but what happened to Levels 2 and 3? Why the delay?"

Smita Gokhale: "That's a fair question. Completing CFA Level 1 while working full-time was already challenging, but my personal responsibilities, including taking care of my younger siblings, made it difficult to commit to the rigorous study schedule required for Levels 2 and 3. Additionally, CFA Level 2 demands an in-depth understanding of financial modeling and derivatives, which require focused preparation.

However, I haven't given up. My plan is to take Level 2 next year, and I am already dedicating time to studying portfolio management and quantitative risk analysis. With a better work-life balance now, I am confident about clearing the next levels."

Interviewer: "That's understandable. Now, tell me about the key challenges you face in your current role as a Risk Manager. Can you share an incident where you had to handle a major risk-related issue?"

Smita Gokhale: "One of the biggest challenges in risk management is ensuring compliance with constantly evolving regulations while balancing business growth. The pressure to meet targets sometimes leads to aggressive lending, which increases credit risk.

One notable incident was when I identified inconsistencies in a high-value loan proposal that had already been cleared at multiple levels. My team flagged discrepancies in the borrower's financials, which hinted at fund diversion. Upon deeper investigation, we discovered that the borrower had inflated revenues and understated liabilities. Based on our risk assessment, we escalated the matter, and the loan was put on hold. Eventually, external auditors confirmed fraudulent activity, preventing a potential NPA situation.

This experience reinforced the importance of due diligence and proactive risk management in banking."

Interviewer: "That's a great example of risk identification. Now, let's switch to a technical scenario. A multinational corporation (MNC) is evaluating the country risk before investing in a foreign subsidiary. Their assessment is based on political stability, GDP growth, inflation, and exchange rate volatility. However, the MNC's bank does not have its own country risk assessment system. As per RBI guidelines, what should the bank do in this case, and what are the implications of a high-risk rating?"

Smita Gokhale: "As per RBI guidelines, if a bank does not have its own country risk assessment system, it should adopt the Export Credit Guarantee Corporation (ECGC)'s country risk classification.

A high-risk rating indicates that the country has elevated political or economic instability, which increases the probability of defaults or financial distress. This necessitates provisions for potential losses, as the bank must maintain additional capital buffers to mitigate risks associated with lending or investment in that country. High-risk ratings may also lead to stricter credit terms, increased due diligence, and higher interest rate spreads to compensate for the additional risk."

Interviewer: "That's correct. Moving on, explain Value at Risk (VaR) and its application in banking risk management."

Smita Gokhale: "Sir, Value at Risk (VaR) is a statistical measure that quantifies the potential loss in the value of a portfolio over a given time frame at a specified confidence level.

For example, if a bank reports a one-day 99% VaR of   ₹10 crore, it means that there is a 99% probability that the bank will not lose more than

₹10 crore in a single day under normal market conditions.

VaR is widely used in banking for market risk assessment, investment portfolio management, and stress testing. It helps banks allocate capital efficiently, determine risk exposure limits, and comply with Basel III capital requirements. However, it has limitations as it does not account for extreme market shocks (tail risk)."

Interviewer: "Well explained. Now, let's analyze a real banking scenario. Assume a bank's loan book consists mostly of floating-rate loans linked to the Repo Rate, while its deposits are primarily in fixed-rate term deposits. Suppose the central bank reduces the Repo Rate from 4% to 3.5% over six months. How will Basis Risk affect the bank's Net Interest Margin (NIM)?"

Smita Gokhale: "Basis Risk occurs when interest rates on a bank's assets and liabilities adjust at different times or to different extents, impacting Net Interest Margin (NIM).

Since the bank's floating-rate loans are tied to the Repo Rate, the interest earned on these loans will decrease almost immediately when the central bank reduces the Repo Rate from 4% to 3.5%.

However, the fixed-rate term deposits remain unchanged because their interest rates are locked in for a fixed period. This creates a timing mismatch where interest income decreases, but the interest expense remains the same, leading to a contraction in NIM.

If the Repo Rate continues to fall, the bank's profitability will be further squeezed, making it imperative for risk managers to hedge against such interest rate mismatches."

Interviewer: "Smita, let's now move towards some more practical lending decisions. Assume a small business owner approaches your bank for a   ₹2 crore loan to scale up operations. While evaluating the character aspect, you discover that their previous venture was shut down due to bankruptcy within two years. The owner insists it was due to external factors beyond their control, though their personal credit history is strong. However, you notice that their business strategies involve speculative investments with high returns. Given this background, how should the bank weigh the character aspect in the credit appraisal process?"

Smita Gokhale: "Sir, character evaluation is a crucial aspect of credit appraisal, as it reflects the borrower's integrity, financial discipline, and ability to manage business risks. While the owner's personal credit history shows a responsible repayment pattern, the fact that their past business collapsed within two years due to bankruptcy raises significant concerns.

Moreover, their inclination towards speculative investments indicates a high-risk appetite, which may not align with the bank's prudent lending practices. Even if external factors contributed to their past failure, a lender must ensure that the borrower has learned from past mistakes and has a sustainable, well-structured business model. Given this, the bank should impose stringent lending conditions, such as higher collateral requirements, risk-based pricing, or even a phased disbursement strategy, to mitigate potential losses. In certain cases, based on further risk assessment, rejection could also be a prudent option."

Interviewer: "Good assessment, Smita. Moving on to global economics—the U.S. President recently imposed tariffs on Canada, Mexico, and China. What impact will this have on both the importing and exporting countries?"

Smita Gokhale: "Sir, tariffs directly influence trade dynamics by making imported goods more expensive for the importing country while reducing demand for exports from the affected nations. In this case, the United States, as the importer, will witness an increase in the cost of imported goods from Canada, Mexico, and China, leading to higher inflationary pressures. Consumers and businesses that rely on imported goods will bear the brunt of these tariffs.

For the exporting countries, these tariffs reduce their competitive edge, leading to a drop in exports, possible trade deficits, and economic slowdowns. China, for instance, may look for alternative markets or focus on domestic demand to counteract reduced U.S. orders. Over time, such tariff policies can trigger retaliatory measures, disrupting global trade and slowing down economic growth."

Interviewer: "That's right. Now, coming back to operational banking—can you tell me, Drawing Power is required to be arrived at based on what?"

Smita Gokhale: "Stock Statement, Sir. The Drawing Power (DP) is calculated based on the current stock statement, which considers the available inventory and receivables after applying the prescribed margin by the bank. It ensures that working capital loans remain within permissible limits based on actual business conditions."

Interviewer: "Correct. Now, let's talk about trade finance. What is an Inland Letter of Credit (LC)?"

Smita Gokhale: "An Inland Letter of Credit is a financial instrument issued for domestic trade transactions where all involved parties are within the same country. It ensures that the seller receives payment once the specified conditions are met, reducing credit risk.

In this arrangement, the buyer's bank issues the LC on behalf of the buyer, committing to pay the seller upon fulfilling the contract terms. It is commonly used in domestic supply chains where large orders require structured payment security."

Interviewer: "That's well articulated, Smita. Before we conclude, I want to ask a personal question. You have faced significant challenges managing both professional and personal responsibilities. What keeps you motivated despite the obstacles?"

Smita Gokhale: "Sir, my biggest motivation is the responsibility I carry towards my younger siblings. Losing my father at an early age forced me to develop resilience, and banking gave me the platform to create a stable financial future for my family. Every promotion, every challenge overcome, and every milestone in my career strengthens my ability to provide for them.

Beyond personal responsibilities, I genuinely enjoy solving complex financial and risk-related problems. The dynamic nature of banking keeps me engaged, and I believe that my ability to analyze risk and ensure financial stability adds value to the bank and its customers. Looking forward, I aspire to grow further in risk management and make impactful contributions to the industry."

Interviewer: "Smita, I appreciate your clarity of thought, technical knowledge, and resilience. Your insights on risk assessment, global trade implications, and lending decisions were impressive. I believe you have the potential to take on higher responsibilities within the bank. Thank you for this engaging discussion, and I wish you the best for your career progression."

Smita Gokhale: "Thank you, Sir. It was a pleasure interacting with you, and I truly appreciate the opportunity to share my thoughts."

Interviewer: "Best of luck, Smita!

• • •

CHAPTER XXI

7 Years in Banking, One Rare Condition, and a Risk Management Masterclass— Neeraj Khanna's Scale 2 Promotion Interview

Interview Snapshot - (Scale I to II)

This interview with Neeraj Khanna is a standout blend of technical rigor, personal resilience, and leadership under pressure. From dissecting cybersecurity threats and compliance challenges to gracefully correcting an NPA inspection error, Neeraj showcases how depth of knowledge and humility can go hand in hand. His unique approach to overcoming prosopagnosia adds a compelling layer to his operational excellence. This isn't just an interview—it's a lesson in how to turn vulnerabilities into strengths and earn respect even when things don't go perfectly. A must-read for every serious candidate.

Candidate Profile: Neeraj Khanna (Assistant Manager, Scale I)

Neeraj Khanna, currently serving as a Scale 1 Officer in Dharwad, Karnataka, has built a strong reputation in banking operations, fraud risk management, and cybersecurity over his 7-year banking career. Originally from Bhopal, Madhya Pradesh, he started as a clerk and rose through the ranks due to his operational excellence and proactive leadership. Certified in CAIIB, Fraud Risk Management, and Digital Banking & Cyber Security, Neeraj has played a key role in minimizing financial risks at the branch level.

He has spearheaded multiple account opening and financial inclusion drives, resulting in over 5,000 new accounts, particularly in rural and underbanked areas. His deep knowledge of regulatory compliance, transaction monitoring, and AML protocols has enhanced operational controls and customer trust.

Neeraj's journey is marked by a rare personal challenge—Prosopagnosia (face blindness), which hinders his ability to recognize faces. This has occasionally led to misunderstandings in customer interactions. However, he compensates by leveraging voice cues, meticulous note-taking, and a heightened focus on detail. Interestingly, this condition has sharpened his skills in identifying data anomalies and fraud indicators.

Aiming for a Scale 2 role in Risk Management or IT Security, Neeraj blends technical acumen with adaptive problem-solving, making him a standout candidate for advancement.

• • •

Setting: "The interview room is formal yet welcoming. A panel of seasoned bankers sits at a long table, their expressions a blend of curiosity and professionalism. Neeraj Khanna, dressed sharply in a navy-blue suit, steps in confidently. His composed demeanor reflects his seven years of experience in banking operations. The lead interviewer, Mr. Rajan, a Senior General Manager, gestures for him to take a seat.

Interviewer (Mr. Rajan): "Good morning, Neeraj. I see from your profile that you've had quite a journey—from starting as a clerk to becoming a Scale 1 Officer in operations. That's commendable. Let's start with something simple. Tell us about yourself—your journey in banking, what drives you, and where you see yourself heading."

Neeraj Khanna: "Good morning, sir, and thank you for the opportunity. My journey in banking began with a strong desire to contribute to financial inclusion and operational excellence. Starting as a clerk taught me the foundational aspects of banking—handling customers, processing transactions, and understanding the intricate balance between compliance and customer service. Over the years, I've specialized in risk management, fraud prevention, and cybersecurity, which aligns with my interest in creating secure banking environments. What motivates me is the dynamic nature of banking—how each day presents new challenges that require quick thinking and adaptability. I've had the privilege of leading account opening camps in rural areas, which has been deeply fulfilling. Seeing the impact of banking services in underbanked communities has reinforced my belief in the transformative power of financial inclusion. My goal now is to move into a role where I can focus more on risk management and compliance, contributing to the bank's strategic efforts in these critical areas."

Interviewer (Ms. Iyer): "That's an inspiring journey, Neeraj. I also read from your promotion form as you have written that you live with Prosopagnosia—face blindness. That's quite rare, especially in a customer-facing role like yours. How do you manage this in your day-to-day work, especially when dealing with regular customers and colleagues?"

Neeraj Khanna: "Yes, ma'am, it's a unique challenge, but over the years, I've developed strategies to manage it effectively. I rely heavily on contextual cues—like voice recognition, specific behavioral traits, and even the way people dress or carry themselves. I also maintain detailed notes about frequent customers, including their banking preferences and key details from our previous interactions. This helps me create a sense of familiarity, even if I can't visually recognize them. Interestingly, while this condition makes facial recognition difficult, it has sharpened my attention to detail in other areas. I've become highly observant when it comes to transactional data and behavioral patterns, which has been particularly useful in fraud detection. In a way, this challenge has honed my analytical skills, allowing me to spot irregularities that might go unnoticed by others."

Interviewer (Mr. Rajan): "That's an admirable way to turn a challenge into a strength. Let's shift gears to fraud prevention, an area you seem to excel in. Suppose you notice a pattern of small but frequent unauthorized transactions across multiple customer accounts—what immediate steps would you take to investigate and mitigate the risk?"

Neeraj Khanna: "In such a scenario, my first step would be to conduct a thorough analysis of the transaction patterns to confirm whether they are indeed unauthorized. I would initiate an internal audit to trace the origin of these transactions, looking for common factors such as the same IP address, similar transaction amounts, or recurring timestamps. If fraud is suspected, I would immediately flag the affected accounts, freeze them temporarily to prevent further losses, and inform the customers involved. Simultaneously, I would work with the IT security team to identify any breaches in the system, such as phishing attacks or malware intrusions. Customer communication is also critical—I would ensure they are informed promptly and provided with guidance on securing their accounts. Finally, I would review the existing fraud detection protocols and recommend enhancements to prevent such incidents in the future. The goal is to act swiftly, minimize financial loss, and strengthen the bank's defenses against similar threats."

Interviewer (Mr. Kapoor): "That's a comprehensive approach. Now, let's talk about the legal aspects of banking. Referring to the banker-customer relationship, if a customer takes a loan from the bank, what is the legal relationship between the bank and the customer?"

Neeraj Khanna: "In the context of a loan, the legal relationship between the bank and the customer is that of a creditor and debtor. The bank, as the creditor, provides funds to the customer with the expectation of repayment under agreed terms, which include interest rates, repayment schedules, and other contractual obligations. This relationship is formalized through a loan agreement, which outlines the rights and responsibilities of both parties. The bank has the legal right to recover the loan amount along with interest, while the customer has the obligation to repay as per the agreed terms."

Interviewer (Ms. Iyer): "Correct. Let's move to operational compliance. Suppose a newly incorporated public limited company approaches you to open an account. What documents would you require to comply with regulatory norms?"

Neeraj Khanna: "For a public limited company, the documentation process is quite thorough to ensure compliance with KYC and regulatory norms. I would require the original Certificate of Incorporation and, in the case of a public company, the Certificate of Commencement of Business. Additionally, I'd need a copy of the Memorandum and Articles of Association, which outline the company's structure and purpose. A Board Resolution authorizing the opening of the account, signed by the chairman of the meeting where the resolution was passed, is also necessary. I'd also request a list of current directors, signed by the chairman, and the latest audited balance sheet along with the profit and loss account. These documents help verify the legitimacy of the company and its financial standing, ensuring that the bank's risk is minimized."

Interviewer (Mr. Rajan): "Good. Now, let's consider a hypothetical situation. Imagine a customer accidentally leaves valuable items at the bank, and they're later found by an employee. What is the bank's legal responsibility in this case?"

Neeraj Khanna: "In such a situation, the bank assumes the role of a trustee, and the customer becomes the beneficiary. The bank has a fiduciary responsibility to safeguard the item until it can be returned to its rightful owner. This means the bank must document the discovery of the item, including details like the date, time, and circumstances under which it was found. Efforts should be made to contact the customer, using available information from the bank's records. If the item remains unclaimed for an extended period, the bank should follow established protocols, which may include handing over the item to the relevant authorities, depending on the nature of the item and internal policies. This approach ensures that the bank fulfills its legal and ethical obligations while maintaining the trust of its customers."

Interviewer (Ms. Iyer): "Moving on to international banking—if ICICI Bank opens a Nostro Account with Bank of America, and HDFC Bank refers to this account for its transactions, what would HDFC Bank call this account?"

Neeraj Khanna: "In this scenario, for ICICI Bank, the account with Bank of America would be called a Nostro Account, as it represents ICICI's account held in a foreign bank. For HDFC Bank, which refers to ICICI's account for its own transactions, it would be termed a Loro Account. Essentially, a Loro Account is "their account with you," referring to another bank's account maintained with a foreign correspondent bank."

Interviewer (Mr. Kapoor): "Excellent. Let's touch on loan security. What is the significance of Full Value Insurance in the context of secured business loans?"

Neeraj Khanna: "Full Value Insurance is crucial because it ensures that the property or asset securing the loan is insured for its complete market value. This is important because, in the event of damage or loss, the insurance coverage should be sufficient to cover the outstanding loan amount. In many cases, an additional margin—typically around 10%—is recommended to account for fluctuations in the asset's value. This provides a cushion that protects the bank's interests, ensuring that the collateral remains adequate to cover the loan even if its market value changes over time."

Interviewer (Mr. Rajan): "Now, let's discuss negotiable instruments. If a bearer cheque is endorsed by a person who subsequently passes away, can their legal heirs complete the transaction?"

Neeraj Khanna: "No, legal heirs cannot complete the transaction in such a case. According to the Negotiable Instruments Act, an endorsement is a personal act that requires the intent of the endorser. Once the person passes away, their legal authority to endorse ceases, and any attempt by legal heirs to complete the negotiation would be invalid. The instrument loses its negotiability through endorsement after the endorser's death."

Interviewer (Ms. Iyer): "My next question for you Neeraj. You've expressed interest in moving into risk management and compliance. However, you've also mentioned limited exposure to retail credit and corporate lending. How do you plan to overcome this gap to become a well-rounded banker?"

Neeraj Khanna: "That's a valid observation, ma'am. While my expertise is rooted in operations, risk management, and cybersecurity, I recognize that a comprehensive understanding of retail credit and corporate lending is essential for career growth. To bridge this gap, I've actively sought opportunities to collaborate with credit officers in my current role. I participate in credit committee discussions to gain firsthand exposure to loan appraisal and underwriting processes. Additionally, I've enrolled in advanced courses focused on credit risk assessment to deepen my theoretical knowledge. My goal is to integrate risk management principles into lending practices, ensuring that credit decisions are both sound and compliant with regulatory guidelines. This proactive approach will help me develop the skills needed to excel in broader banking roles."

Interviewer (Mr. Rajan): "Neeraj, we'll now move on to some conceptual questions based on banking inspections and credit mechanisms. Let's begin with loan inspections. Could you explain the frequency of inspections required for Non-Performing Asset (NPA) accounts and why they are critical?"

Neeraj Khanna: "Certainly, Sir. For Non-Performing Asset (NPA) accounts, inspections are conducted annually to evaluate the loan recovery process and determine the next steps if the situation worsens. The idea is to ensure that the bank's exposure is minimized, and potential risks are identified in time."

Interviewer (Mr. Rajan): "Correcting Neeraj: Not exactly, Neeraj. While you're right about the intent of inspections, the frequency for NPAs is more rigorous. Inspections for such accounts must be conducted at least half-yearly, given the higher risk they pose. In fact, if the situation deteriorates further, the frequency of inspections can increase to allow for timely corrective measures. This helps the bank monitor the asset closely and take prompt action to recover dues."

Neeraj nods, acknowledging the correction with a composed expression.

Interviewer (Ms. Iyer): "Let's discuss end-use monitoring. Why is post-disbursement inspection critical, especially for movable assets, and what does it entail?"

Neeraj Khanna: "Post-disbursement inspection is crucial because it verifies that the loan disbursed by the bank has been utilized for its intended purpose. For movable assets, this inspection should ideally be conducted within one month of disbursement. It ensures that the asset exists, has been procured, and is being used appropriately. Additionally, the inspection details are recorded in the bank's inspection register, which helps maintain proper documentation and compliance."

Interviewer (Mr. Kapoor): "Good. Now, based on follow-up functions, could you elaborate on how detecting early warning signals helps in credit risk management?"

Neeraj Khanna: "Sir, Detecting early warning signals is a proactive approach in credit risk management. It involves identifying signs of potential financial distress in the borrower's operations. These signals could be delayed repayments, declining turnover, frequent overdraft requests, or irregularities in operational performance. Recognizing these indicators early allows the bank to intervene promptly—through restructuring loans, increasing monitoring, or initiating recovery processes—thus minimizing the risk of default and protecting the bank's financial interests."

Interviewer (Ms. Iyer): "Moving to the Kisan Credit Card (KCC), what is the primary objective of the scheme, and how does it benefit farmers?"

Neeraj Khanna: "Mam, The primary objective of the Kisan Credit Card scheme is to provide need-based and timely credit support to farmers for their cultivation and non-farm activities. It offers short-term credit for crop production, allied activities like dairy and poultry farming, and other agricultural needs. The scheme is flexible and cost-effective, helping farmers manage seasonal financial requirements efficiently. It also includes provisions for non farm credit needs, making it comprehensive for rural credit support."

Interviewer (Mr. Rajan): "Very well. Now, let's test your understanding of loan follow-up responsibilities. How does the continuous assessment of outstanding loans contribute to the bank's risk mitigation strategies?"

Neeraj Khanna: "Sir, Continuous assessment of outstanding loans helps the bank correlate the loans with the borrower's current asset status. It ensures that the loan proceeds are effectively contributing to asset creation or business growth, as per the sanctioned terms. This assessment allows the bank to identify any discrepancies early, such as underutilization of funds or deviation from the sanctioned purpose, and take corrective actions before the situation escalates. It ultimately safeguards the bank's credit portfolio and reduces the likelihood of loans turning into NPAs."

The panel exchanges thoughtful glances, appreciating Neeraj's depth of knowledge despite the minor slip earlier.

Interviewer (Mr. Rajan): "Neeraj, we've covered a broad range of topics today—from fraud prevention and operational efficiency to credit risk and compliance. We appreciate your clarity of thought, attention to detail, and the way you handled both technical and situational questions. Even though there was a slight error regarding the NPA inspection frequency, you accepted the correction gracefully, which speaks to your openness to learning—a crucial quality for leadership roles."

Neeraj Khanna: "Thank you, sir. I genuinely appreciate the feedback. This session has been insightful, and I'm grateful for the opportunity to reflect on areas where I can improve. I look forward to applying these learnings to enhance my contributions to the bank."

Interviewer (Ms. Iyer): "That's the spirit, Neeraj. Adaptability and continuous learning are the hallmarks of a strong banker. We'll conclude the interview here, and you'll be informed of the results soon. All the best!"

Neeraj stands, offers a polite smile, and exits the room with renewed confidence.

• • •

CHAPTER XXII

When Empathy Meets Execution: A Banker's Unseen Edge in MSME Credit Decisions

Interview Snapshot - (Scale II to III)

Explore the interview that goes beyond textbook answers—where MSME lending meets emotional grit. Raghavendra Shetty's journey is packed with real-world credit risk handling, tech-driven lending strategies, and people-first financial literacy models. His poised response to a high-stakes ethical dilemma and approach to sudden customer defaults reveal the kind of thinking interview panels admire. More than just a promotion interview, this conversation is a playbook of practical wisdom, laced with personal resolve and visionary leadership in digital credit transformation.

Candidate Profile: Raghavendra Shetty (Manager, Scale II, MSME Department)

Raghavendra Shetty, currently serving as a Scale II Manager in the MSME Department at Hubballi Zonal Office, Karnataka, brings nine years of diverse banking experience with a strong focus on MSME credit and business development. A Certified Financial Planner with advanced credentials from IIM Calcutta in Digital Transformation & FinTech, he has consistently delivered innovative lending solutions to underserved business communities. His efforts have led to a 35% growth in the MSME portfolio of the Hubballi region within just two years.

Having worked across rural banking, priority sector lending, and digital banking, Raghavendra excels in blending traditional banking with modern tech-driven approaches. He has conducted over 50 financial literacy workshops and played a key role in implementing AI-based credit scoring systems. Additionally, he's a published author and runs a personal finance YouTube channel, aiming to empower individuals through financial awareness.

However, behind his professional success lies a difficult personal challenge. Raghavendra's younger brother struggles with a gambling addiction, causing significant financial and emotional strain on the family. As the eldest son,

Raghavendra bears the responsibility of repaying debts and supporting his parents. Despite these pressures, he remains committed, channeling his resilience into professional excellence—making him a strong, well-rounded candidate for future leadership roles.

•••

Interviewer: "Good morning, Mr. Shetty. Please have a seat. How are you feeling today?"

Raghavendra Shetty: "Good morning, sir. Thank you. I'm feeling confident and prepared."

Interviewer: "That's great to hear. Confidence is the first step to success. Before we dive into the technical aspects, why don't you start by telling me a bit about yourself and your journey in the banking sector?"

Raghavendra Shetty: "Certainly, sir. I hail from a small town in Karnataka and currently serve as a Scale II Manager in the MSME Department at Hubballi Zonal Office. Over the past nine years, I've had the opportunity to work in diverse roles, including rural branch management, priority sector lending, and digital banking services. My current role involves evaluating and sanctioning MSME loans, developing financial literacy programs for small business owners, and promoting digital credit solutions. I've also authored two books on personal finance and run a YouTube channel where I guide individuals on financial planning."

Interviewer: "Impressive, Mr. Shetty. Managing a ₹100 crore MSME loan portfolio while contributing to financial literacy is commendable. Now, let me shift gears a bit. Considering your extensive experience in MSME lending, could you explain what cluster financing is and how it benefits the MSE sector?"

Raghavendra Shetty: "Certainly, sir. Cluster financing is a strategic approach where banks cater to the financial needs of recognized MSE clusters. This approach allows banks to provide a full-service model to businesses within a specific geographic or industry cluster. The benefits include better risk assessment due to the availability of comprehensive data, efficient monitoring, cost reduction, and the ability to offer tailored financial products. This approach fosters stronger relationships with businesses and promotes economic growth within the cluster."

Interviewer: "That's a well-articulated response. Now, considering your background in digital banking, can you explain the Trade Receivables Discounting System (TReDS) and its significance for MSMEs?"

Raghavendra Shetty: "Absolutely. TReDS is an electronic platform designed to facilitate the financing of trade receivables for MSMEs. It enables MSMEs to discount their invoices and access funds promptly, improving their cash flow. The system brings together MSMEs, corporate buyers, and financiers on a single platform, enhancing transparency and reducing payment delays. This mechanism not only strengthens MSME liquidity but also instills greater payment discipline among large corporates."

Interviewer: "Excellent. Let's delve into a hypothetical scenario now. Suppose you're handling a case where an MSME client, who has been a loyal customer with an impeccable repayment record, suddenly defaults on a significant loan installment. How would you approach this situation?"

Raghavendra Shetty: "In such a scenario, my first step would be to initiate a direct conversation with the client to understand the root cause of the default. It's essential to differentiate between temporary cash flow issues and deeper financial distress. I would review their recent financial statements, analyze market conditions affecting their business, and assess any operational challenges. Based on this assessment, I could propose restructuring the loan, offering a temporary moratorium, or exploring additional credit support if viable. The goal would be to support the client while safeguarding the bank's interests."

Interviewer: "That's a balanced approach, showcasing both empathy and prudence. Moving on, during your career, you've conducted several financial literacy workshops. What strategies have you found most effective in engaging small business owners?"

Raghavendra Shetty: "Engaging small business owners requires a blend of simplicity and relevance. I focus on practical, real-life examples that resonate with their daily operations. Interactive sessions, case studies, and success stories from within their community create a relatable learning environment. Additionally, I emphasize digital tools and resources that can simplify their financial management, making the sessions both informative and actionable."

Interviewer: "Well-articulated, Mr. Shetty. On a related note, could you explain the conditions under which an asset is classified as current?"

Raghavendra Shetty: "Certainly. An asset is classified as current if it meets any of the following conditions: it is expected to be realized, sold, or consumed within the normal operating cycle, which is typically 12 months; it is due to be settled within 12 months from the reporting date; it is held primarily for trading purposes; or it is cash or a cash equivalent, including bank deposits without any lien or restrictions."

Interviewer: "Excellent clarity. Now, let's pivot slightly. After seeing your promotion form where you mentioned you faced some family challenges, how have you managed to maintain professional excellence while dealing with such personal adversity?"

Raghavendra Shetty: "Thank you for acknowledging that, sir. Managing personal and professional responsibilities simultaneously has been challenging. I rely on disciplined time management, setting clear priorities, and maintaining a strong support system both at work and home. My commitment to my professional duties provides a sense of purpose and stability, which has been instrumental in navigating personal hardships."

Interviewer: "That's truly inspiring, Mr. Shetty. Your resilience is commendable. Now, as we move ahead, here's a twist. Imagine you're suddenly appointed as the head of a new digital transformation initiative for MSME lending across your bank. What would be your first three strategic steps to ensure its success?"

Raghavendra Shetty: "In such a scenario, my first step would be to conduct a comprehensive needs assessment, identifying gaps in the current MSME lending processes and understanding customer pain points. Next, I would focus on stakeholder alignment, involving cross-functional teams to ensure buy-in and collaborative execution. Finally, I would prioritize technology integration, selecting digital tools that enhance efficiency, improve customer experience, and ensure robust risk management. Continuous feedback loops and agile project management would be key to adapting and refining the initiative."

Interviewer: "That's a well-thought-out strategy. Mr. Shetty, your responses have been insightful, reflecting both depth of knowledge and practical experience. Let's continue with a few more questions to explore your perspective further."

Interviewer: "Which accounting concept assumes that an entity will continue its operations into the foreseeable future?"

Raghavendra Shetty: "That would be the Going Concern Concept. It is the fundamental assumption that an entity will continue its operations and not liquidate in the near future, allowing assets and liabilities to be recorded based on their ongoing value."

Interviewer: "Correct. Now, can you explain the Cash Budget Method (CBM) and its relevance in working capital financing?"

Raghavendra Shetty: "The Cash Budget Method is used to sanction short-term loans where repayment is planned in suitable installments. It is particularly effective for businesses dealing with seasonal products, construction projects, or order-based activities. This method focuses on cash flow patterns, with the peak cash deficit determining the total working capital finance provided by the bank. It helps in efficient liquidity management and is widely popular in developed countries."

Interviewer: "Well-explained. Moving on, what is Break-Even Analysis (BEA), and how is it useful in project appraisals?"

Raghavendra Shetty: "Break-Even Analysis is a technique used to determine the sales volume at which total costs equal total revenue, indicating no profit or loss. It helps businesses understand the relationship between costs, sales volume, and profits. In project appraisals, it aids in assessing profitability, cost structures, and the financial viability of new ventures. Capital-intensive projects often have a higher break-even point due to significant fixed costs."

Interviewer: "Good. Let's discuss Public-Private Partnership (PPP) models in infrastructure lending. Can you name some common PPP models?"

Raghavendra Shetty: "Yes, sir. Some common PPP models include BOT (Build-Operate-Transfer), BOO (Build-Own-Operate), and BOOT (Build-Own-Operate-Transfer). These models facilitate collaboration between the government and private sector, enabling efficient infrastructure development through shared risks and resources."

Interviewer: "Excellent. Lastly, how is Drawing Power (DP) calculated, and why is it significant in working capital finance?"

Raghavendra Shetty: "Drawing Power is calculated based on periodic stock and receivable statements submitted by the borrower. The bank scrutinizes these statements, adjusting for non-moving stocks and overdue receivables to ensure accuracy. DP determines the maximum limit up to which a borrower can utilize funds under a working capital facility, ensuring that the credit exposure is backed by sufficient current assets."

Interviewer: "Thank you, Mr. Shetty. Your in-depth knowledge and practical insights are impressive. Before we conclude, here's an unexpected twist: Imagine you receive an offer to join a global fintech startup as the Head of Credit Risk, offering a significantly higher salary and international exposure. However, this means leaving your current role and responsibilities behind. How would you approach this decision?"

Raghavendra Shetty: "That's an intriguing scenario. I would start by evaluating the alignment of this opportunity with my long-term career goals and personal values. While financial benefits and international exposure are appealing, I would consider the impact on my professional growth, family responsibilities, and current commitments. I believe in making decisions that offer holistic growth, balancing professional aspirations with personal fulfillment and social contributions."

Interviewer: "A thoughtful and balanced approach, Mr. Shetty. This concludes our interview. Thank you for your candid responses and insightful discussion. It's been a pleasure interacting with you."

Raghavendra Shetty: "Thank you, sir. It's been an honor to participate in this discussion."

• • •

CHAPTER XXIII

Beyond the Branch: How One Rural Banker Mastered High-Stakes Questions with Unshakable Clarity

Interview Snapshot - (Scale I to II)

This interview brings forward an emotionally layered and technically rich dialogue where rural banking meets real-world complexity. Anand Krishnan's answers reflect a rare combination of grit, ethical clarity, and deep subject knowledge—ranging from financial analytics and audit to trade finance and SARFAESI procedures. The way he navigates personal adversity while maintaining professional composure adds depth. You'll walk away with more than just model answers—you'll gain perspective on handling high-pressure questions with confidence, clarity, and character that truly resonates with panels.

Candidate Profile: Anand Krishnan (Assistant Manager, Scale I)

Anand Krishnan, a Scale 1 Officer currently posted in Dhrol village, Jamnagar district, Gujarat, has built a strong foundation in rural and agricultural banking over seven years of service. Originating from Thrissur, Kerala, Anand began his career as a clerk and rose through the ranks due to his diligence, grassroots understanding, and problem-solving skills. In his current role, he manages rural credit portfolios, including Kisan Credit Cards, SHG financing, crop insurance, and financial inclusion drives.

Anand is particularly noted for his empathetic engagement with farmers, women-led SHGs, and local artisan groups, promoting digital banking and improving financial literacy in underbanked regions. He has facilitated over ₹30 crore in agricultural loans, led 50+ literacy camps, and reduced loan delinquency rates by 20% through field-based borrower education.

Despite facing emotional stress due to a personal family controversy—his father, a retired government employee, was recently convicted in a corruption case. This situation has caused emotional stress and occasional prejudice from colleagues and customers. Despite this Anand remains steadfast in his ethical approach and professional integrity. His resilience, people-centric mindset, and commitment to inclusive banking have earned him deep respect in the community.

Keen to grow further, Anand aims to transition into a Scale 2 role with broader exposure to MSME and corporate lending, while continuing to bridge the urban-rural divide in financial services delivery.

• • •

Interviewer: "Good morning, Anand. Before we begin, tell me a bit about yourself, your journey in banking so far, and what drives you in your role."

Anand Krishnan: "Good morning, sir. I started my career as a clerk and gradually worked my way up to a Scale 1 Officer role, primarily focusing on retail and rural banking in Dhrol Village, Gujarat. Over the last five years, I have been deeply involved in agricultural finance, financial inclusion initiatives, and risk management in rural credit. What motivates me the most is the impact we create in empowering rural communities—whether through Kisan Credit Cards, SHG financing, or promoting digital banking awareness."

Interviewer: "That's commendable. Working in rural banking requires both patience and innovation. Before we discuss technical aspects, I'd like to ask a personal question. Given the challenges in your personal life, particularly your father's situation, how have you managed to maintain your professional integrity and reputation despite any societal biases?"

Anand Krishnan: "It has undoubtedly been a tough phase, sir. Banking is built on trust, and I understand that personal credibility is as important as professional competence. I have made it a point to be transparent in my dealings, strictly adhere to ethical banking practices, and ensure that my work speaks for itself. I also proactively engage with customers, address concerns openly, and maintain professional conduct to dispel any doubts about my integrity."

Interviewer: "That's a mature approach. Now, let's dive into your expertise. Given your experience in rural banking, suppose a major bank is planning to implement a new training program focused on advanced financial analytics for its employees, ranging from junior analysts to senior managers. What training methods would you recommend for maximum effectiveness?"

Anand Krishnan: "I would suggest a multi-tiered approach to cater to different experience levels. Junior analysts would benefit from hands-on technical training using case studies and simulation-based learning to understand the mechanics of financial analytics. Mid-level officers should have interactive workshops and group discussions to apply analytics to real-world banking decisions. Senior managers, on the other hand, should focus on strategic implementation through scenario-based training and data-driven decision-making simulations. This blended learning approach ensures that each group gains practical, applicable knowledge suited to their roles."

Interviewer: "That's an insightful framework. Now, moving on to risk control—what are the key objectives of Concurrent Audit in banks, and how does it enhance financial governance?"

Anand Krishnan: "Concurrent Audit plays a crucial role in banking operations by ensuring compliance, preventing fraud, and mitigating risks. Its primary objectives revolve around acting as an administrative support system that ensures adherence to established procedures. It also involves verifying that records and registers are maintained according to prescribed standards, thereby upholding the integrity of financial documentation. Concurrent audits help identify compliance gaps early on, which aids in preventing potential frauds and operational inefficiencies. Additionally, they reduce the time lag between a transaction and its independent review, enabling real-time risk detection. By proactively addressing these compliance risks, concurrent audits enhance governance frameworks, ensuring that any discrepancies are promptly corrected before they develop into more significant operational issues."

Interviewer: "That's a well-structured answer. Now, let's test your knowledge on financial crimes. A property dealer purchases a ₹2 million property for ₹1 million, secretly passing the balance to the seller. After holding the property for a while, the launderer then sells it for its full ₹2 million value. What is this method of money laundering called?"

Anand Krishnan: "This technique is known as Value Tampering. It is a method where assets are intentionally misrepresented in value during transactions to legitimize illicit money. Criminals manipulate the purchase price, underreporting it initially and later selling at the true market value, thereby justifying the illegal funds as legitimate profits from the sale."

Interviewer: "Correct. Let's talk about international banking now. Suppose an Asian bank refers to the USD account of a European bank that is held with a U.S. bank. What type of account does this refer to, and why is it significant in international banking?"

Anand Krishnan: "This is a LORO Account. In correspondent banking, a LORO account refers to an account that a bank holds with another bank but is referred to by a third party. In this case, the Asian bank is referring to the USD account of the European bank that is maintained with a U.S. bank. LORO accounts are crucial in international transactions as they facilitate efficient cross-border payments, collections, and liquidity management among financial institutions across different jurisdictions."

Interviewer: "That's absolutely right. Now, let's discuss trade finance. What is a letter of credit that allows pre-shipment financing and storage of goods in the name of the bank called?"

Anand Krishnan: "That would be a Green Clause Letter of Credit. This type of LC extends beyond standard trade financing by allowing sellers to obtain advance payments before shipment and also finance storage costs. The issuing bank holds control over the goods through a trust receipt or warehouse receipts, ensuring additional security while enabling smoother trade transactions."

Interviewer: "Excellent, Anand. One last question before we conclude. Given your limited exposure to MSME and corporate lending, how do you plan to bridge this knowledge gap if you are promoted to Scale 2 and transferred to a semi-urban or urban branch?"

Anand Krishnan: "While my primary expertise lies in rural finance, I have a strong foundation in credit risk assessment and financial inclusion, which are transferable skills in MSME lending. To bridge the gap, I would proactively take up structured learning through internal bank training programs and industry certifications. Additionally, I would seek mentorship from senior credit officers, participate in credit committee discussions, and closely analyze MSME loan proposals to develop a hands-on understanding of structuring and underwriting business loans. My adaptability and commitment to continuous learning would help me transition effectively into MSME and corporate lending."

Interviewer: "That's the right approach, Anand. Let's move on to some situational and technical aspects now. Suppose you are managing a team where one of your associates seems disengaged and lacks motivation. To begin addressing this, you informally ask her about her job satisfaction concerning safety, social interaction, self-respect, and opportunities for growth. What theory of motivation are you applying in this scenario?"

Anand Krishnan: "In this situation, the manager is most likely applying Maslow's Hierarchy of Needs. According to Maslow, human needs are structured in a hierarchical manner, starting from basic physiological needs to safety, social belonging, self-esteem, and finally self-actualization. By informally discussing aspects like job security, social connections, and growth opportunities, the manager is trying to identify which level of needs the associate feels are unmet. Understanding this helps tailor motivational strategies to address specific gaps, whether it's providing a sense of security, enhancing peer interactions, or offering professional development opportunities."

Interviewer: "That's a precise explanation. Now, shifting to negotiable instruments, can you explain the conditions that make an instrument negotiable?"

Anand Krishnan: "Certainly. The conditions of negotiability are fundamental in the realm of banking and finance. First, the instrument should be freely transferable, either by delivery or by endorsement and delivery, depending on its type. Second, the holder in due course — someone who obtains the instrument for value, in good faith, and without notice of any defects — should not be affected by any defects in the title of the transferor. This ensures that the instrument remains secure and reliable for subsequent holders. Third, such a person can sue upon the instrument in their own name, providing legal enforceability and protection for genuine transactions. These conditions uphold the integrity and fluidity of negotiable instruments in the financial system."

Interviewer: "Well articulated. Let's discuss mortgages now. Which type of mortgage allows the mortgagor to continue enjoying physical possession of the property?"

Anand Krishnan: "That would be a Usufructuary Mortgage. In this arrangement, while the ownership rights are mortgaged to the lender, the mortgagor retains possession and the right to enjoy the property's benefits. The lender does not receive regular payments but may have the right to collect rents or profits generated by the property until the debt is repaid. This type of mortgage is common in agricultural contexts where the borrower continues to cultivate the land or manage the property while it serves as collateral for the loan."

Interviewer: "Correct. Now, in legal and financial contexts, what do we call the process where a person transfers their rights or benefits to another person?"

Anand Krishnan: "The process is known as Assignment. In banking, assignment typically involves transferring rights or interests from one party to another, such as the assignment of loan receivables, insurance policies, or lease agreements. The assignor transfers the benefits or obligations to the assignee, who then becomes the new rightful holder of those rights. Assignments are crucial in credit transactions, securitization, and debt recovery processes, ensuring flexibility and liquidity in financial markets."

Interviewer: "Excellent. Let's now discuss the enforcement of security interests under the SARFAESI Act. What are the key procedures involved when a secured creditor takes possession of a property?"

Anand Krishnan: "Sir, the enforcement of security interest under the SARFAESI Act, 2002 is a structured process designed to enable secured creditors to recover dues without court intervention. Firstly, when a secured creditor takes possession of a property, they must prepare an inventory of the property and entrust it to an authorized officer or a person appointed by the creditor. This ensures accountability and proper documentation.

If the property is subject to speedy or natural decay, or if the cost of maintaining it exceeds its value, the authorized officer can proceed to sell the property immediately to prevent further loss. Additionally, the officer must publish a possession notice in two leading newspapers, including one in the local vernacular, to ensure transparency and public awareness of the action.

When it comes to the sale of the secured asset, if the offered price is below the reserve price, the officer can still sell it at the lower price, but this requires the consent of both the borrower and the secured creditor. This provision balances the interests of the creditor while protecting the borrower from potential undervaluation. The SARFAESI framework thus promotes efficient recovery mechanisms while ensuring fairness and legal compliance."

Interviewer: "Impressive, Anand. Your answers reflect a deep understanding of both theoretical concepts and practical banking operations. Considering your strong rural banking background, how do you envision applying these regulatory frameworks and financial principles if you transition into urban or corporate banking roles?"

Anand Krishnan: "I believe that while the scale and complexity of operations differ between rural and urban banking, the core principles of risk management, compliance, and customer-centric service remain universal. My experience in rural banking has given me a strong foundation in credit assessment, financial literacy promotion, and grassroots-level risk management. In an urban or corporate banking environment, I would apply these principles to more complex credit portfolios, focusing on structured financial analysis, regulatory compliance, and strategic customer relationship management.

Moreover, my background in rural credit risk management equips me with a proactive approach to monitoring and mitigating risks, which is equally critical in MSME and corporate lending. I am eager to complement this with formal training in corporate finance and exposure to diversified lending scenarios, thereby broadening my professional horizon while maintaining my commitment to ethical banking practices."

Interviewer: "That's the right mindset. Anand, your journey reflects resilience, adaptability, and a strong ethical compass—qualities that are invaluable in leadership roles. It was a pleasure speaking with you today. We'll be in touch soon regarding the next steps in your promotion process."

Anand Krishnan: "Thank you very much, sir. I truly appreciate the opportunity to discuss my experiences and aspirations. I look forward to contributing more significantly to the bank's growth in the future."

• • •

CHAPTER XXIV

From PMFBY Gaps to Digital Disconnects: This Interview Redefines Rural Banking Realities

Interview Snapshot - (Scale I to II)

This interview offers a compelling mix of field-tested insights and brutally honest self-reflection. From decoding loan eligibility for landless farmers to explaining how PMFBY struggles on the ground, Devendra tackles nuanced questions with practical clarity. His responses to digital banking challenges, compromise settlements, and rural NPAs reveal not just technical know-how, but a strategic mindset rooted in real experiences. What truly sets this apart is how he owns his flaws, turning them into opportunities for growth—something every future officer must master.

Candidate Profile: Devendra Chauhan, (Scale 1, Agriculture Field Officer (AFO))

Devendra Chauhan, a Scale 1 Agriculture Field Officer (AFO) with five years of service, is currently posted in the rural regions of Ambala, Haryana. Originally from Sri Ganganagar, Rajasthan, he has built a strong track record in agricultural and rural lending. Certified in Agricultural Finance, NPA Management, and both JAIIB and CAIIB, Devendra has disbursed over ₹60 crore in farm loans, processed 500+ MUDRA applications, and spearheaded multiple financial literacy campaigns in remote villages.

He is well-versed in crop cycle-based credit planning, KCC distribution, PMFBY claims, and NABARD-linked schemes. His practical knowledge in loan recovery and risk mitigation has led to a 20% drop in agri-loan delinquencies in his region. Known for his analytical thinking and ground-level problem-solving, Devendra also tailors credit structures to suit seasonal farming incomes.

Despite these strengths, Devendra grapples with a personal challenge—his short temper and aggressive communication style. He has faced complaints from customers regarding harsh interactions, prompting him to actively work on developing better interpersonal and conflict-resolution skills.

Devendra aspires to become a Scale 2 Officer, either as a Senior AFO or Branch Manager. His long-term goal is to shape policy in agricultural finance, contributing to inclusive growth and rural development at a strategic level.

• • •

Interviewer: "Good morning, Mr. Chauhan. It's a pleasure to have you here today. To start, could you please share a bit about your journey from Sri Ganganagar to becoming an Agriculture Field Officer in Ambala?"

Devendra: "Good morning. Thank you for having me. I hail from Sri Ganganagar, Rajasthan, where agriculture is a predominant occupation. My upbringing in this environment instilled in me a deep appreciation for farming and rural development. After completing my studies, I joined the bank as an Agriculture Field Officer and have been serving in the rural regions of Ambala, Haryana, for the past five years. My role has primarily involved facilitating agricultural loans, promoting financial literacy among farmers, and implementing various government schemes to enhance rural credit access."

Interviewer: "That's commendable. Given your extensive experience, how do you approach the assessment of creditworthiness for farmers, especially those without traditional collateral?"

Devendra: "Assessing creditworthiness in such scenarios requires a different approach. I focus on understanding the farmer's crop patterns, yield history, and market linkages. Additionally, evaluating their participation in government schemes, such as the Pradhan Mantri Fasal Bima Yojana (PMFBY), provides insights into their risk mitigation strategies. Building strong relationships and trust within the farming community also aids in accurate assessments."

Interviewer: "Speaking of government schemes, can loans given to landless individuals engaged solely in allied activities be classified under the Small and Marginal Farmers (SMF) category of priority sector lending?"

Devendra: "Yes, according to the Reserve Bank of India's guidelines, bank loans up to ₹2 lakh extended to individuals solely engaged in allied activities, without any accompanying landholding criteria, are eligible for classification under the SMF category of priority sector lending. This inclusion aims to support those involved in activities like dairy, poultry, and fisheries, ensuring they have access to necessary credit facilities."

Interviewer: "That's correct. Now, let's consider a hypothetical scenario: If a student avails two education loans, one for ₹12 lakhs and another for ₹18 lakhs, how would these be treated under priority sector lending norms?"

Devendra: "Post September 4, 2020, if the aggregate sanctioned limit of multiple education loans to a single borrower exceeds ₹20 lakh, all such loans sanctioned after this date become ineligible for priority sector lending classification. Therefore, in this scenario, both loans would not qualify under the priority sector. Banks are advised to obtain declarations from borrowers regarding any existing education loans from other banks and to independently verify this information to ensure compliance."

Interviewer: "Exactly. Moving on, the Kisan Credit Card (KCC) scheme has been pivotal in providing timely credit to farmers. Could you elaborate on the recent extensions or modifications to the interest subvention scheme associated with KCCs?"

Devendra: "Certainly. The Reserve Bank of India has extended the interest subvention scheme for short-term crop loans through KCCs. Under this scheme, farmers are eligible for a 2% interest subvention, and an additional 3% prompt repayment incentive, effectively reducing the interest rate for timely repayers. This initiative aims to encourage prompt repayments and ensure the availability of affordable credit to the farming community."

Interviewer: "That's insightful. In your opinion, how effective has the KCC scheme been in promoting financial inclusion among small and marginal farmers?"

Devendra: "The KCC scheme has significantly enhanced financial inclusion by simplifying the credit delivery mechanism. It offers farmers flexible and timely access to credit for their cultivation and other needs. The streamlined process and reduced documentation have particularly benefited small and marginal farmers, enabling them to meet their financial requirements without resorting to informal lending sources."

Interviewer: "Indeed, the scheme has been transformative. Now, on a more personal note, it's been noted that you've faced challenges related to communication styles with customers. How have you been addressing this aspect of your professional development?"

Devendra: "I acknowledge that my communication style has, at times, been perceived as harsh, leading to customer complaints. To address this, I've been actively working on improving my interpersonal skills. I've attended workshops on effective communication and conflict resolution and have been seeking feedback from colleagues and customers to better understand and rectify my shortcomings. My goal is to foster a more empathetic and customer-friendly approach in all interactions."

Interviewer: It's commendable that you're taking proactive steps in this area. Reflecting on your experience, can you share an instance where your intervention led to a significant positive outcome for a farmer or the community?

Devendra: "Certainly. There was a case where a group of small farmers was struggling due to a lack of awareness about crop insurance schemes. I organized a series of financial literacy camps to educate them about the benefits and enrollment processes of the PMFBY. As a result, many farmers enrolled in the scheme, and when unforeseen weather conditions affected their crops, the insurance payouts provided them with much-needed financial relief. This experience reinforced the importance of awareness and education in empowering the farming community."

Interviewer: "That's a powerful example of the impact of financial literacy. Considering the PM-KISAN scheme introduced in 2019, which provides   ₹6,000 per year to farmers in three equal installments, what are your views on such income support initiatives? Do you think they risk making farmers complacent?"

Devendra: "Income support schemes like PM-KISAN offer immediate financial relief to farmers, helping them manage short-term expenses and invest in essential inputs. While there's a concern that such assistance might lead to complacency, I believe that when combined with initiatives promoting sustainable farming practices and capacity building, these schemes can enhance productivity. The key lies in ensuring that support is coupled with education and resources that encourage long-term self-reliance."

Interviewer: "That's a balanced perspective. Lastly, looking ahead, what strategies would you propose to further reduce non-performing assets (NPAs) in the agricultural loan segment?"

Devendra: "To mitigate NPAs in agricultural lending, it's crucial to implement robust credit appraisal mechanisms that consider the unique challenges of farming. Regular monitoring of loan utilization, coupled with flexible repayment schedules aligned with crop cycles, can aid in timely recoveries. Additionally, promoting crop diversification and providing farmers with market linkage support can enhance their income stability, reducing the likelihood of defaults. Engaging with farmers through continuous financial literacy programs also empowers them to manage loans more effectively."

Interviewer: "Mr. Chauhan, you've shared some excellent insights so far. Now, let's delve into a few more critical areas before we conclude. Let's start with Self-Help Groups (SHGs). Can you outline the eligibility criteria for an SHG to avail of bank loans?"

Devendra: "To be eligible for bank loans, an SHG must be in active existence for at least six months, as per its books of accounts, rather than just the date of opening a savings bank account. The SHG must also practice the 'Panchasutras,' which include regular meetings, regular savings, internal lending, timely repayments, and proper bookkeeping. Additionally, the SHG should qualify under the grading norms set by NABARD, and in the future, if SHG Federations are formed, they can conduct the grading exercise to support banks. Even defunct SHGs can be eligible for credit if they have been revived and have remained active for a minimum of three months."

Interviewer: "Very well explained. Now, let's talk about loan restructuring. Which concessions can lead to a facility being classified as restructured?"

Devendra: "A facility is classified as restructured if the borrower is granted certain concessions. These include a reduction in the principal installment amount or the amount payable at maturity, deviating from the original loan agreement. It can also occur if the interest rate is lowered from the originally contracted terms, or if there is a reduction or forgiveness of accrued interest. Additionally, a facility is considered restructured if there is a deferral or extension of interest or principal payments, including interest capitalization."

Interviewer: "Correct. Now, let's consider a situation where a borrower negotiates a settlement with the bank and offers to pay an amount that is less than the total due under the debt account, and the bank accepts it as full and final settlement. What is this process called?"

Devendra: "Sir, that process is known as a Compromise Settlement. It is a negotiated resolution where the borrower and the bank agree to settle the dues for an amount lower than the total outstanding, leading to the closure of the debt account. This is often done in cases where full recovery is not feasible, and a one-time settlement is considered a better alternative."

Interviewer: "Absolutely right. Moving on to government schemes, you've worked extensively with PMFBY, NABARD, and MUDRA. From your experience, what are some challenges in implementing PMFBY at the ground level?"

Devendra: "PMFBY has provided risk coverage to farmers, but certain challenges persist. A major issue is delayed claim settlements due to dependency on crop-cutting experiments (CCEs) and lengthy state government processes. This reduces farmers' trust in the scheme. Lack of awareness is another problem, as many small farmers do not fully understand the scheme and its benefits, leading to lower enrollment. Additionally, yield estimation issues sometimes result in disputes, as crop-cutting experiments do not always reflect actual losses accurately. While technology like satellite imagery is being integrated, its ground-level implementation is still evolving. To improve the scheme, greater transparency, faster processing, and enhanced farmer education are essential."

Interviewer: "Excellent points. Let's talk about digital banking in rural areas. Despite major efforts toward financial inclusion, what are some persistent challenges in rural banking digitalization?"

Devendra: "Digital banking in rural areas has improved, but there are still significant barriers. Limited digital literacy prevents many customers from confidently using mobile banking and digital transactions. Poor internet connectivity in remote villages further restricts access. Another major concern is cybersecurity—many rural customers fall victim to fraud, making them reluctant to use digital banking services. Additionally, cash dependency remains strong, as rural economies are largely informal and prefer cash transactions. Expanding banking correspondent (BC) networks and conducting digital literacy programs can help bridge this gap."

Interviewer: "That's an insightful analysis. Before we conclude, I'd like to ask one final question: Given your experience and aspirations, if promoted, what would be your first key initiative as a Scale II Officer in a rural or semi-urban branch?"

Devendra: "My first priority would be to enhance credit outreach while ensuring better asset quality. I would strengthen loan monitoring mechanisms to reduce NPAs in agriculture and MSME loans. Conducting financial literacy and digital banking awareness programs would also be a key focus to encourage responsible borrowing and digital adoption. Additionally, I would work on innovative lending models like Farmer Producer Organizations (FPOs) and Joint Liability Groups (JLGs) to facilitate easier credit access for small farmers. Leveraging data-driven decision-making in loan appraisals would help in better risk assessment, and I would also prioritize improving customer service and grievance redressal to strengthen trust among rural customers."

Interviewer: "That's a solid plan, Mr. Chauhan. It has been a pleasure discussing these topics with you. Your knowledge and practical experience in agricultural finance, loan recovery, and digital banking will certainly be valuable in your next role. Thank you for your time, and I wish you all the best for your career progression!"

Devendra: "Thank you so much! This discussion has been truly insightful, and I appreciate the opportunity. I look forward to applying these learnings in my future role."

• • •

CHAPTER XXV

Boardroom Pressure, Forex Puzzles, and ESG Dilemmas—This Scale IV Interview Has It All

Interview Snapshot - (Scale III to IV)

This interview is a masterclass in handling high-stakes technical questions with composure and clarity. It reveals how a seasoned banker navigates complex topics like trade finance, ESG lending, export delays under LCs, and RBI's evolving forex regulations—all while addressing personal leadership gaps. With layered questions that simulate real-world challenges, including INR-denominated trade, diamond dollar accounts, and green energy financing, the interview offers a blueprint for delivering sharp, strategic answers under pressure—just the edge you need to face your own interview panel.

Candidate Profile: Suraj Nandekar, (Senior Branch Manager, Scale 3)

Suraj Nandekar, a Senior Branch Manager (Scale 3) in Corporate & Forex Banking, brings 12 years of specialized experience from industrial corridors across Maharashtra. Currently posted in Pimpri-Chinchwad near Pune's manufacturing hub, he has successfully onboarded over ₹500 crore in corporate accounts and issued 300+ Letters of Credit, positioning himself as a trusted partner for trade finance and forex advisory. A CDCS-certified professional, Suraj is known for his structured approach to import-export finance, forex hedging strategies, and working capital solutions for large industrial clients.

Under his leadership, the branch's forex income surged by 40%, supported by his deep understanding of cross-border transactions and treasury operations. He's also played a key role in MSME financing under CGTMSE and interest subvention schemes, facilitating over ₹250 crore in disbursements.

Despite his success, Suraj faces a personal challenge—public speaking and negotiating under pressure, especially in high-stakes corporate meetings. Recognizing this gap, he has proactively enrolled in an executive program to enhance his communication and boardroom presence.

With strengths in trade finance, corporate lending, and process optimization, Suraj aspires to lead a regional corporate banking division at Scale 4 and eventually transition into treasury or international banking roles. His strategic mindset and commitment to growth set him apart.

• • •

Interviewer: Welcome, Mr. Nandekar. You have had an impressive career in corporate and forex banking, particularly in industrial lending and trade finance. Before we get into specifics, tell me a bit about yourself, your journey in banking so far, and what drives you toward this promotion.

Suraj Nandekar: Thank you. I began my banking journey 12 years ago and have spent the majority of my career handling corporate and industrial accounts, with a strong focus on forex services and trade finance. Currently, as a Senior Branch Manager at Pimpri-Chinchwad, I have worked extensively with large industrial clients, facilitated structured trade finance solutions, and expanded forex transactions at my branch by 40%. My passion lies in enabling businesses to optimize their banking operations, and I see this promotion as a step toward leading a larger team and contributing more strategically in corporate banking and treasury operations.

Interviewer: That's a strong foundation. Before we dive into technical aspects, I'd like to start with something personal which you have mentioned in your promotion form. Public speaking and high-stakes negotiations are areas you've been working on improving. Can you share a situation where you struggled with this, and what steps you're taking to overcome it?

Suraj Nandekar: Certainly. There was an instance where I had to present a forex hedging strategy to a panel of CFOs from multiple auto-component manufacturers. While I had deep technical knowledge, I struggled to convey the key takeaways in a structured, impactful manner. I realized that technical expertise alone isn't enough—communication is equally critical. Since then, I have enrolled in an executive leadership program to refine my public speaking and negotiation skills. I am now practicing concise articulation of complex financial strategies, using case studies and interactive discussions to engage clients more effectively.

Interviewer: That's a great approach. Now, let's discuss trade finance. Considering your CDCS certification and experience, how do you ensure that the Letter of Credit (LC) issuance process is both secure and efficient, particularly in today's evolving regulatory landscape in India?

Suraj Nandekar: LC issuance must balance speed, accuracy, and compliance. Given RBI's focus on AML measures and fraud prevention, we follow strict due diligence protocols, ensuring KYC norms, UCP 600 guidelines, and FEMA regulations are adhered to. To enhance efficiency, we have integrated automated LC processing, reducing errors and transaction turnaround times. Additionally, we proactively educate clients on structuring LCs to minimize risks, such as incorporating clauses to prevent discrepancies and using digital trade finance solutions for faster document exchange.

Interviewer: You've facilitated over 300 LCs for businesses. If a large manufacturing client comes to you with a request for a ₹50 crore LC, but their credit rating has recently declined, how would you assess their risk and structure the LC accordingly?

Suraj Nandekar: Risk assessment would begin with analyzing their financial health, recent cash flows, and order book strength. If their rating decline is due to temporary working capital strain, we could explore collateral-backed LCs or standby LCs from parent companies. Another option is to issue an LC with a shorter validity period, reducing risk exposure. Additionally, I would recommend a confirmed LC backed by a stronger international bank if the beneficiary demands more security. If their fundamentals are weak, we would reassess their eligibility for non-funded credit facilities or suggest structured trade finance alternatives.

Interviewer: Good. Moving to corporate lending, what key parameters do you analyze when assessing a company's working capital requirement for a ₹200 crore industrial term loan?

Suraj Nandekar: For large industrial term loans, key parameters include current and projected cash flows, DSCR (Debt Service Coverage Ratio), EBITDA trends, industry outlook, and promoter credentials. We also assess collateral strength, existing debt obligations, and receivable cycles. Given RBI's guidelines, we stress-test financials against adverse conditions such as raw material price fluctuations or forex volatility. If liquidity risk is high, structuring the loan with balloon repayments or moratorium periods can be considered to align with revenue cycles.

Interviewer: Let's discuss a hypothetical scenario. Suppose an MSME client under CGTMSE has defaulted on a ₹5 crore loan due to a sudden economic downturn. What steps would you take to recover dues while ensuring regulatory compliance?

Suraj Nandekar: First, we would conduct a detailed viability assessment to see if restructuring under RBI's stressed asset framework is an option. If the business is fundamentally sound but facing short-term liquidity issues, we could offer a one-time restructuring plan with revised repayment terms. If revival is unlikely, invoking CGTMSE guarantee claims would be necessary, ensuring all procedural compliances are met to avoid claim rejection. Simultaneously, recovery actions like SARFAESI proceedings may be initiated if collateral exists. Throughout, I would ensure strict adherence to RBI's Fair Practices Code to maintain ethical lending practices.

Interviewer: Moving to compliance, recent RBI guidelines emphasize ESG (Environmental, Social, and Governance) risks in corporate lending. How do you see ESG factors impacting future credit decisions in India?

Suraj Nandekar: ESG is becoming a key determinant in corporate lending, especially post-RBI's emphasis on sustainable finance. Banks are now integrating carbon footprint assessments, green compliance, and governance standards into risk evaluations. Companies failing ESG benchmarks might face higher borrowing costs or restricted credit access. For instance, industries with high environmental liabilities (like chemical manufacturing) may require stricter risk mitigations. As ESG regulations evolve, we will likely see banks offering preferential rates for green projects, similar to priority sector lending benefits.

Interviewer: What are the major regulatory challenges banks face when handling forex transactions, especially in light of RBI's recent policy changes?

Suraj Nandekar: RBI has tightened forex transaction monitoring to prevent illicit fund flows. Key challenges include stricter KYC/AML norms, real-time trade settlement compliances, and volatility in external commercial borrowings (ECB) regulations. With liberalized remittance scheme (LRS) limits revised and restrictions on certain capital account transactions, banks must continuously update their compliance frameworks. The introduction of RBI's Centralized KYC Registry and AI-driven transaction monitoring is helping mitigate risks, but it also demands higher operational efficiency from banks handling forex transactions.

Interviewer: Speaking of digital banking, how has automation transformed trade finance operations, and what innovations do you foresee in India's trade finance ecosystem?

Suraj Nandekar: Automation has significantly reduced LC processing times and enhanced transaction security through blockchain-based trade finance platforms. The introduction of SWIFT gpi tracking has made international payments more transparent. Going forward, I foresee AI-driven trade finance risk assessment, real-time document authentication via blockchain, and integration of India's TReDS (Trade Receivables Discounting System) with global payment networks. These innovations will improve liquidity for exporters and reduce dependency on traditional LC-backed transactions.

Interviewer: Now, let's shift to leadership and negotiation. You're managing high-value industrial accounts. What's your approach to handling a high-stakes negotiation with a corporate CFO who demands lower forex rates than your bank's threshold?

Suraj Nandekar: Negotiations require a balance between client retention and bank profitability. First, I would analyze their annual forex turnover and profitability contribution to our bank. If they are a key client, I would explore offering volume-based incentives or structured hedging solutions instead of outright rate discounts. If a rate reduction is non-viable, I'd highlight our faster trade execution, advisory strength, and lower transaction costs to justify our pricing. If required, I'd escalate to treasury desks for structured forex deals that optimize their cost while maintaining bank margins.

Interviewer: Suraj, you've demonstrated a deep understanding of corporate banking, trade finance, and risk management. Now, let's challenge your ability to think strategically in high-pressure situations. Imagine this—your branch has recently facilitated a high-value export transaction for a large auto component manufacturer, but the foreign buyer is delaying payment beyond the agreed LC terms. The exporter is pressuring the bank for immediate resolution. How would you handle this situation within RBI's trade finance regulations?

Suraj Nandekar: In such a scenario, my first step would be to evaluate whether the LC is confirmed or unconfirmed. If it is a confirmed LC, the confirming bank must honor the payment obligation regardless of the buyer's delay. However, if the LC is unconfirmed, I would investigate the reason behind the payment delay—whether it is due to financial distress, regulatory issues, or documentary discrepancies. Given that RBI regulations permit export realization extensions up to 270 days under FEMA guidelines, I would explore whether the exporter can benefit from this provision. If immediate liquidity is a concern, we could assist them with bill discounting against the export LC, subject to credit approval. Additionally, if the transaction is covered under ECGC, I would guide the exporter in filing a claim while simultaneously coordinating with the overseas bank and buyer to resolve the delay amicably. If the delay appears to be intentional or signals potential default, we may escalate the issue through diplomatic banking channels and, if necessary, consider legal arbitration mechanisms available under international trade laws.

Interviewer: Mr.Nandekar, as you know, India's external trade has been impacted by fluctuating forex reserves and policy changes. Given the RBI's recent initiatives to promote INR-denominated trade settlements, how can banks encourage corporate clients to shift from USD-based invoicing to rupee-based trade?

Suraj Nandekar: Sir, to promote INR-denominated trade settlements, banks must educate corporate clients on the benefits of reducing exposure to USD volatility, minimizing conversion costs, and enhancing transactional stability. The RBI has already established Vostro accounts in several partner countries, which facilitates direct rupee transactions and removes the need for intermediary currencies like the USD. I would work closely with exporters and importers to assess whether their counterparties in eligible nations, such as Russia and UAE, are willing to adopt this mechanism. Additionally, I would leverage structured advisory sessions to help businesses understand the long-term financial advantages of INR invoicing. Another key enabler would be offering customized forex hedging solutions that provide businesses confidence in rupee transactions. For instance, rupee forward contracts and cross-currency derivatives can be structured to mitigate potential forex risk fluctuations. By integrating these approaches and collaborating with government trade bodies, banks can drive greater adoption of INR-denominated trade.

Interviewer: Shifting gears to corporate lending, let's say an industrial client is seeking a   ₹300 crore term loan for a green energy transition project under the RBI's new Sustainable Finance Framework. What key factors would you consider while structuring this loan?

Suraj Nandekar: Sir, Under the Sustainable Finance Framework, the RBI has incentivized lending to green projects through priority sector classification and concessional interest rates. While structuring this loan, I would focus on several key factors. First, I would evaluate the project's financial viability, analyzing projected cash flows, DSCR, and cost-benefit analysis over its lifecycle. Second, I would assess regulatory compliance and environmental impact, ensuring that the project aligns with India's sustainability goals, such as the National Green Hydrogen Mission or renewable energy policies. Risk mitigation would also be crucial—this could involve securing partial credit guarantees from green finance institutions or leveraging carbon credit monetization strategies to enhance repayment capacity. Furthermore, given the long gestation period of green projects, structuring the loan with a phased disbursement schedule and flexible repayment options, such as balloon repayments, would be prudent. I would also explore whether the client qualifies for government incentives, such as viability gap funding (VGF), which could further strengthen the project's financial feasibility.

Interviewer: Now Do you know what are Diamond Dollar Accounts (DDA), and why are they relevant to the Indian banking and trade finance ecosystem?

Suraj Nandekar: Yes Sir, Diamond Dollar Accounts (DDA) are specialized forex accounts introduced by the RBI to facilitate seamless international trade transactions for exporters in the gems and jewelry sector. These accounts allow eligible exporters to maintain foreign currency balances in USD, EUR, or GBP, enabling them to conduct trade-related transactions without the need for frequent currency conversions. The primary advantage of DDAs is that they help exporters mitigate forex fluctuation risks while ensuring smoother transactions in a highly volatile global market. Given that India is one of the largest diamond processing and export hubs, these accounts play a crucial role in ensuring liquidity and cost efficiency for industry players. Moreover, RBI guidelines mandate that funds maintained in DDAs must be used strictly for trade-related purposes, such as procuring raw diamonds or meeting working capital requirements. As a banker, my role would involve ensuring compliance with FEMA guidelines while advising clients on efficient forex management using DDAs.

Interviewer: Incoterms 2020 play a critical role in structuring international trade contracts. Can you explain the significance of Incoterms in trade finance and give an example of how a specific Incoterm affects risk allocation in an export transaction?

Suraj Nandekar: Sir, Incoterms 2020, established by the International Chamber of Commerce (ICC), define the responsibilities of buyers and sellers in international trade transactions, particularly in terms of risk transfer, shipping obligations, and cost allocations. These terms are essential in structuring trade finance agreements as they influence the pricing, documentation, and risk assessment of a transaction. For example, under the FOB (Free on Board) Incoterm, the seller's responsibility ends once the goods are loaded onto the vessel, and the risk transfers to the buyer at that point. This means that if any damage occurs after loading but before arrival at the destination, the buyer bears the loss. On the other hand, under the CIF (Cost, Insurance, and Freight) term, the seller is responsible for freight and minimum insurance coverage until the goods reach the buyer's port. This distinction directly impacts how banks structure LC terms, insurance requirements, and risk mitigation strategies. When advising clients, I ensure that they choose Incoterms that align with their financial and logistical capabilities to minimize risks and optimize trade financing options.

Interviewer: As we conclude, let's discuss a recent policy shift. The RBI has increased the risk weightage on unsecured loans for NBFCs and banks. How do you see this impacting corporate lending, and what strategies should banks adopt in response?

Suraj Nandekar: Sir, The RBI's decision to increase the risk weightage on unsecured loans is aimed at controlling excessive leverage and maintaining financial stability. This move will lead to tighter credit conditions, as banks and NBFCs will need to allocate higher capital provisions against unsecured exposures. Consequently, borrowing costs for corporates relying on unsecured loans will rise, making collateralized lending more attractive. To adapt to this change, banks should prioritize secured lending through instruments such as term loans, LC-backed facilities, and structured finance solutions. Additionally, risk-based pricing strategies should be refined, where interest rates are adjusted based on borrower creditworthiness and financial stability. Another crucial approach would be enhancing co-lending partnerships between banks and NBFCs, ensuring risk-sharing while maintaining asset quality. Lastly, credit insurance products and guarantees from institutions like ECGC can be leveraged to mitigate potential defaults in unsecured lending. By implementing these strategies, banks can sustain growth in corporate lending while ensuring regulatory compliance and prudent risk management.

Interviewer: Suraj, this has been an insightful discussion. Your expertise in corporate and forex banking, combined with your ability to think strategically in complex scenarios, makes you a strong contender for this promotion. As you move forward, refining your leadership and negotiation skills will be key, especially in high-stakes boardroom discussions. Before we wrap up, do you have any final thoughts on your aspirations in the banking industry?

Suraj Nandekar: Thank you Sir! My goal is to contribute at a larger strategic level in corporate and forex banking, ensuring businesses get innovative financial solutions while maintaining robust risk management. With India's banking landscape evolving rapidly—especially in digital trade finance and sustainable banking—I am eager to take on greater leadership responsibilities and drive impactful initiatives. I believe that with continuous learning and effective leadership, I can contribute significantly to strengthening India's position in global trade finance.

Interviewer: That's a commendable vision. Best of luck with your promotion journey, Suraj. Looking forward to seeing you take on bigger roles in the Indian banking sector.

• • •

CHAPTER XXVI

Tech, Trust, and Turnarounds: An IT Manager's Playbook for Leading Through Change and Conquering his Scale 3 Promotion

Interview Snapshot - (IT Manager, Scale II to III)
This interview with Vijay Kumar Gupta is a masterclass in navigating the intersection of technology, leadership, and crisis management in banking. From decoding POP3 and IPv6 to managing data breaches, vendor risks, and real-time system failures, Vijay's responses demonstrate clarity, composure, and conviction. His ability to turn resistance into results and setbacks into strategic wins makes this an essential read. If you're aiming to elevate your interview game with tech-driven insights and leadership depth, this one delivers the blueprint.

Candidate Profile - Vijay Kumar Gupta (IT Manager, Scale II)
Vijay Kumar Gupta, currently serving as an IT Manager (Scale 2) at State Bank, brings 6 years of dynamic experience in banking technology and innovation. A Certified Blockchain Expert (CBE), he played a pivotal role in developing the bank's AI-powered chatbot and was honored with a national-level award for innovation in digital banking. Despite his professional success, Vijay faces internal resistance from senior management when proposing advanced tech solutions, which leads to workplace frustration and self-doubt.

• • •

Interviewer: "Good morning, Mr. Gupta. Congratulations on being shortlisted for this promotion interview."

Vijay Kumar Gupta: "Good morning, Sir. Thank you very much. I'm honored to be here."

Interviewer: "You've had an impressive career so far—six years in banking as specialist IT Officer, leading AI initiatives, and even winning a national banking award. Let me start by asking, what inspired you to pursue a career blending IT and banking?"

Vijay Kumar Gupta: "Sir, while many of my peers opted for software MNCs, I was drawn to the banking sector because it offered the unique opportunity to apply technology in ways that directly impact millions of lives. As an IT Officer in a bank, I could combine my technical skills with a sense of public purpose—building solutions that improve financial inclusion, customer service, and operational efficiency. The challenge of modernizing legacy systems and driving digital transformation from within the system truly inspired me to choose this path."

Interviewer: "That's an excellent perspective. Let's move to a challenge you've faced. As I can read from the challenges section of your promotion form, you have written that you've experienced resistance from senior management regarding advanced technologies. How have you tackled this issue?"

Vijay Kumar Gupta: "Indeed, Sir, resistance was challenging. When I proposed deploying advanced data analytics tools, I encountered skepticism about cost and utility. To address this, I showcased a pilot project with clear metrics on operational efficiency and customer satisfaction improvements. While it didn't completely eliminate resistance, it helped gain some key stakeholders' confidence. I've learned that persistence, backed by data, eventually breaks down barriers."

Interviewer: "That's commendable. Speaking of IT expertise, can you explain the difference between a hub, a switch, and a router, and the layer at which a bridge operates in the OSI model?"

Vijay Kumar Gupta: "Certainly, Sir. A hub operates at the physical layer and simply broadcasts data to all connected devices. A switch operates at the data link layer and forwards data based on MAC addresses, ensuring more efficient data transfer. A router works at the network layer, connecting multiple networks and managing traffic using IP addresses. A bridge also operates at the data link layer, connecting two network segments and filtering traffic based on MAC addresses."

Interviewer: "Perfect. Now let's dive into a topic from your domain. Can you tell us about POP3 and how it differs from IMAP?"

Vijay Kumar: "POP3, or Post Office Protocol version 3, is an email protocol that retrieves emails from a server and downloads them to a local device, often deleting them from the server after download. In contrast, IMAP, or Internet Message Access Protocol, allows users to manage emails directly on the server, enabling synchronization across multiple devices. POP3 is suitable for limited storage scenarios, whereas IMAP is ideal for modern, multi-device environments."

Interviewer: "Good explanation. Let's take a practical scenario. Suppose your Regional/Zonal Office has outdated technology, and the management is reluctant to upgrade. How would you convince them to implement IPv6, considering its complexity?"

Vijay Kumar Gupta: "Sir, I'd begin by highlighting the limitations of IPv4, such as address exhaustion, and the benefits of IPv6, including its vast address space and improved security features. I'd present a phased transition plan, ensuring minimal disruption and showcasing long-term cost savings. Additionally, I'd back the proposal with industry trends and case studies of successful IPv6 migrations to build a compelling business case."

Interviewer: "Strategic thinking—well done. Since you've worked on AI-based chatbots, tell me, what potential do you see for AI in rural banking?"

Vijay Kumar Gupta: "AI can revolutionize rural banking by offering voice-based chatbots in regional languages, enhancing financial literacy, and simplifying processes like account opening or loan applications. It can also help banks predict credit needs based on data patterns, enabling timely interventions. However, user education and infrastructure development are key to unlocking its full potential."

Interviewer: "That's insightful. Let's add some complexity. Imagine a major cybersecurity breach hits your branch's server, and customer data is at risk. How would you handle this crisis?"

Vijay Kumar Gupta: "Sir, my first step would be to immediately isolate the affected systems to prevent further damage. Next, I'd activate the bank's incident response team and notify the cybersecurity cell. Customers would be informed transparently about the breach and advised on preventive measures. Concurrently, I'd initiate an investigation to identify the breach's root cause and implement corrective actions to strengthen our defenses."

Interviewer: "Excellent crisis management approach. Vijay, What has been your most memorable moment in the bank so far?"

Vijay Kumar Gupta: "Sir, winning the national-level banking award for innovation in digital banking was a proud moment for me. It was not just a recognition of my work but also a testament to the potential of our bank to lead in technology-driven banking solutions."

Interviewer: "Moving forward, Mr. Gupta, Let me throw some scenarios at you. Ready?"

Vijay Kumar Gupta: "Absolutely, Sir. I'm eager to take on more challenges."

Interviewer: "Good. Here's a pressing issue. Imagine a major technical failure in the core banking system causes downtime across all branches and digital platforms for hours. Customers are growing restless, and the leadership demands immediate solutions. How would you handle this situation to minimize customer impact, ensure quick restoration of services, and prepare a detailed report for the leadership and regulators?"

Vijay Kumar Gupta: "Sir, the first step would be to activate the bank's Business Continuity Plan (BCP) and Disaster Recovery (DR) setup. I'd communicate transparently with branch managers and customers through all available channels, providing regular updates to manage expectations. Simultaneously, the IT team would work on isolating the issue and coordinating with service providers for swift restoration. A detailed post-incident analysis would be compiled, identifying the failure's root cause and recommending enhancements to the existing systems to avoid recurrence. Timely updates to regulators would also ensure compliance."

Interviewer: "Solid plan. But here's my perspective—transparency with customers should go beyond updates; a token gesture like waiving late fees or extending deadlines for critical transactions could help restore trust post-crisis. Don't you think so?"

Vijay Kumar Gupta: "Absolutely, Sir. Such customer-centric initiatives would indeed help rebuild confidence and mitigate dissatisfaction."

Interviewer: "Now for something strategic. The bank plans to onboard a new IT vendor for implementing an AI-based fraud detection system. During due diligence, you notice gaps in the vendor's data protection policies and regulatory compliance. How would you evaluate the risk, suggest mitigations, and ensure the bank's interests are safeguarded in the agreement?"

Vijay Kumar Gupta: "Sir, I'd first quantify the identified risks using a risk assessment framework. For mitigation, I'd recommend specific clauses in the service agreement, such as penalties for non-compliance, regular third-party audits, and adherence to the bank's security protocols. Additionally, I'd involve legal and compliance teams to ensure the contract covers all regulatory aspects. If the risks remain substantial, I'd explore alternative vendors or suggest enhancements to the vendor's policies before onboarding."

Interviewer: "A structured approach. What if the vendor resists implementing the suggested changes?"

Vijay Kumar Gupta: "In that case, Sir, I'd escalate the matter to leadership with a comparative risk analysis, emphasizing the importance of prioritizing regulatory compliance over convenience."

Interviewer: "Fair enough. Let's tackle one final challenge. An audit reveals discrepancies in the data generated by the bank's core banking system, affecting critical reports submitted to regulators. As the IT Manager, how would you identify the root cause, ensure data integrity, and prevent such issues in the future?"

Vijay Kumar Gupta: "Sir, I'd begin with a comprehensive audit of the core banking system logs to trace the discrepancies. Simultaneously, I'd engage with the software vendor to understand potential system vulnerabilities. To ensure data integrity, I'd implement real-time reconciliation tools and cross-validation mechanisms. For prevention, I'd recommend periodic data quality checks, user training on system usage, and robust change management protocols to handle updates without disrupting data accuracy."

Interviewer: "Excellent. Ensuring data integrity is paramount in an era where data drives decision-making. Mr. Gupta, let's conclude with a personal question. What keeps you motivated despite facing challenges like resistance to innovation and technical crises?"

Vijay Kumar Gupta: "Sir, I believe challenges are opportunities to grow. Knowing that my efforts contribute to the bank's progress and customer satisfaction keeps me motivated. Also, the trust my team and colleagues place in me drives me to keep innovating and overcoming hurdles."

Interviewer: "A great mindset to have. Vijay, imagine you're no longer in your current role but mentoring a young IT manager facing the same challenges you've described. What's the one piece of advice you'd give to them?"

Vijay Kumar Gupta: "I'd tell them to never lose sight of their vision for innovation, even when faced with resistance. Persistence, backed by data and clear communication, eventually wins over doubters. But most importantly, they must stay grounded and open to feedback—it's a collaborative effort."

Interviewer: "Wise words, Mr. Gupta. You've handled this interview exceptionally well. I look forward to seeing you bring more innovative solutions to our bank. Thank you for your time."

• • •

CHAPTER XXVII

Insider Reveals: Why Most Bankers FAIL Their AGM Promotion – But This Chief Manager Cracked It Like a Pro!

Interview Snapshot - (Scale IV to V)

This interview delivers a masterclass in high-stakes corporate banking—packed with sharp, scenario-based answers on trade finance, FEMA compliance, overdue export bills, and forensic scrutiny of red-flagged transactions. Nilesh's ability to handle intense questioning on forex structuring, RBI regulations, and credit stress scenarios is matched by his vulnerability in owning a personal speech challenge with grace and strategy. What makes this interview unmissable is how it blends technical brilliance with the human side of leadership under pressure—something every serious candidate can learn from.

Candidate Profile: Nilesh Patwardhan, (Scale IV, Chief Manager)

Nilesh Patwardhan, currently a Scale IV Chief Manager at Madurai Main Branch, is a seasoned banker with 18 years of diverse experience across corporate credit, forex operations, SME lending, and branch leadership. Originally from Nashik, Maharashtra, he has transformed the forex landscape of his branch by increasing business 120-fold through focused engagement with Madurai's NRI community. His strategic use of trade finance, structured credit, and customer-centric solutions has positioned his branch among the top corporate performers.

Nilesh holds certifications in CAIIB, JAIIB, Certified Credit Professional, and CDCS, equipping him with deep expertise in loan structuring, risk assessment, and international trade transactions. With over ₹1,500 crore in corporate credit exposure under his belt and four Best Manager Awards, his analytical rigor and leadership are well recognized within the bank.

Behind this professional excellence lies a deeply personal challenge—Nilesh lives with a speech impairment (stammering), which impacts high-stakes verbal communication. Rather than allowing this to hinder him, he has developed a strength in structured documentation and data-driven presentations. He also actively works with a speech therapist to improve fluency.

Now preparing for Scale V (AGM), Nilesh aspires to lead zonal or corporate banking initiatives, with a long-term vision of shaping policy in SME, forex, and trade finance.

• • •

Interviewer: "Welcome, Mr. Patwardhan. Before we dive into banking and finance, tell us a little about your journey in banking. What motivated you to pursue this career, and how has your experience at Madurai Main Branch shaped your leadership approach?"

Nilesh: "Thank you. My journey began 18 years ago when I joined the bank as a probationary officer. Coming from Nashik, I was initially more exposed to retail banking. But as I progressed, I developed a strong inclination toward corporate finance, forex, and trade banking. My tenure at Madurai Main Branch was particularly transformational. I realized the potential of the NRI community there and leveraged it to expand our forex and remittance business significantly. I strongly believe in structured decision-making, risk assessment, and data-driven strategies, which have helped me turn around underperforming portfolios."

Interviewer: "Now, Given your extensive experience in corporate credit and forex, can you share an instance where you handled a challenging corporate credit proposal that had high risk, but you successfully structured it into a viable deal?"

Nilesh: "Certainly. One such case involved an engineering goods exporter struggling with cash flow mismatches. The company had bulk orders but faced delays in export payments. Traditional working capital limits were insufficient due to fluctuating cash cycles. The challenge was structuring a funding solution that balanced risk and liquidity.

After detailed due diligence, I proposed a factoring arrangement combined with a standby LC-backed facility. We onboarded a reputed international factoring agency to take over the receivables risk while structuring a working capital limit against confirmed LCs. This solution mitigated payment default risk, improved liquidity, and ensured smoother cash flows. The account is now one of our top-performing SME clients."

Interviewer: "Excellent. Now, let's test your conceptual clarity. Suppose you're reviewing a ₹500 crore mid-corporate proposal, and the latest balance sheet shows a sudden 35% jump in receivables but no proportional increase in revenue. How would you analyze this situation?"

Nilesh: "A sudden spike in receivables without revenue growth is a potential red flag. My approach would be:

- Ageing Analysis of Receivables: Are the receivables from new customers, or is there a growing backlog?
- Related Party Transactions: Is there a possibility of evergreening or artificial sales?
- Revenue Recognition Practices: Any changes in revenue booking methods?
- Liquidity Stress Test: Can the company sustain working capital without additional borrowings?
- Customer Profile Scrutiny: Are top customers facing financial distress?

If these checks indicate window dressing or stressed collections, I would seek clarifications from the company, stress-test their cash flows, and restructure credit limits cautiously."

Interviewer: "Assume you have approved a large MSME credit limit of ₹150 crore based on strong projected growth. Six months later, the client reports a 20% drop in sales due to unexpected market conditions. How would you handle this situation?"

Nilesh: "First, I would assess whether the decline is temporary or structural. If it's temporary, I would explore:

- Short-term restructuring: Extending repayment tenure
- Additional working capital support: Subject to viability
- Alternative revenue sources: Exploring new geographies or customer segments

If the decline is structural (due to competition, regulatory impact, etc.), I would consider:

- Reducing exposure gradually to minimize risk
- Insisting on additional collateral or personal guarantees
- Encouraging business diversification

The key is proactive monitoring and risk mitigation, ensuring that we don't let a short-term crisis turn into an NPA."

Interviewer: "RBI has recently tightened regulations on group exposure limits for corporate lending. How does this impact mid and large corporate borrowers?"

Nilesh: "The revised guidelines restrict single borrower and group borrower exposure limits, reducing banks' risk concentration. Impacts include:

- Diversification of borrowing sources: Corporates will seek funding from multiple banks/NBFCs
- Stronger risk assessment: Banks must avoid excessive exposure to a single entity
- Higher compliance monitoring: Ensuring adherence to Large Exposure Framework (LEF)

This change forces disciplined borrowing and strengthens financial stability, though it may push some large borrowers toward bond markets or alternative financing sources."

Interviewer: "With your expertise in forex, how would you structure a foreign currency loan for a corporate client importing machinery from Germany?"

Nilesh: "The best approach would be an ECB (External Commercial Borrowing) facility or a Buyers' Credit LC. Steps include:

- Determining the optimal currency: EUR vs. USD, based on interest rates and exchange rate stability
- Interest Rate Hedging: Using swaps to manage rate fluctuations
- Forward Cover: Mitigating forex volatility risks
- Repayment Structuring: Matching cash flows to the company's revenue cycle

The key is to minimize forex exposure risk while keeping borrowing costs low."

Interviewer: "As an AGM, you will handle high-value credit decisions. How do you balance business growth with risk management?"

Nilesh: "My approach follows a three-pronged strategy:

- Risk-Based Lending – Ensuring sector-specific credit assessments
- Early Warning Systems – Identifying potential stress signs

- Portfolio Diversification – Avoiding overexposure to high-risk sectors

The goal is to expand lending while ensuring asset quality remains intact."

Interviewer: "You have a remarkable career trajectory, but we also understand you face a personal challenge—your speech impairment. How do you ensure that it does not impact your role in corporate negotiations and high-stake meetings?"

Nilesh: "I acknowledge that verbal fluency can sometimes be a challenge, but I have developed structured communication techniques to compensate.

- Data-Driven Presentations – Letting numbers speak for me
- Pre-Structured Written Briefs – Sharing concise documentation before meetings
- Focused One-on-One Interactions – Reducing group pressure in discussions
- Professional Speech Training – Continually working on improvement

My belief is that clarity in thought and execution matters more than verbal fluency, and I have consistently delivered results that speak louder than words."

Interviewer: "Nilesh, your responses so far have been impressive. You have demonstrated a strong grasp of corporate credit, forex management, and compliance. Before we conclude, let's delve into a few more practical and conceptual aspects of your future role."

Interviewer: "Suppose a mid-sized export company approaches you for an export bill discounting facility, but you find that they have been placed under RBI's Exporters' Caution List. How will you handle this situation?"

Nilesh: "Being on RBI's Exporters' Caution List raises a red flag regarding the company's past transactions and compliance history. My approach would be:

- Understand the reason for the listing – If it is due to pending export realization, I would request documentary proof of corrective actions.
- Verify ECGC Approval – If the client is seeking credit insurance, I would check whether ECGC has granted any coverage despite the caution list.
- Obtain RBI Clearance – In cases where legitimate reasons exist, I would guide them on how to apply for specific approval from RBI for

transactions.

- Mitigate Risk – If permitted, I would structure the facility with additional safeguards, such as a confirmed LC from a prime bank, tighter payment terms, and personal guarantees.

If the risk remains high or compliance is unclear, I would decline the facility to protect the bank's exposure while advising the client on rectifying their regulatory status."

Interviewer: "Many corporate clients look for hedging strategies to mitigate forex risk. If a corporate client importing machinery wants to hedge against USD-INR volatility, what strategy would you recommend?"

Nilesh: "Hedging decisions should be based on the client's risk appetite, cash flow certainty, and market outlook. Possible strategies include:

- Forward Contracts – If the client wants a fixed rate and expects INR depreciation, I'd suggest a forward contract to lock in the exchange rate.
- Options Contracts – If flexibility is needed, a foreign exchange option (call option) can provide downside protection without limiting upside gains.
- Currency Swaps – If they have existing dollar-denominated borrowings, I'd suggest a swap to optimize interest and forex exposure.
- Natural Hedging – If the company has export earnings in USD, internal netting can reduce risk without derivatives.

My final recommendation would align with the company's business model and cash flow cycles to ensure cost-effective risk management."

Interviewer: "Assume you notice an increase in overdue export bills in your branch. What steps would you take to rectify the situation and ensure compliance with FEMA regulations?"

Nilesh: "Overdue export bills can indicate payment delays, documentation issues, or counterparty risk. Immediate steps would be:

- Segregate accounts – Identify whether delays are due to genuine commercial reasons or customer negligence.
- Follow-up with clients – Contact exporters for immediate updates and corrective actions.
- Escalate high-risk cases – If the delay exceeds nine months, I would flag it for RBI reporting under FEMA and ensure proper documentation.

- Adjust Limits – If a pattern emerges, I may reduce working capital limits or insist on LCs instead of open accounts.
- Strengthen Monitoring – Implement stricter follow-up mechanisms, including a Due Date Register, to prevent future overdue instances.

Preventive action ensures reduced compliance risk, avoids FEMA violations, and protects the bank from potential NPAs."

Interviewer: "You are handling a large LC issuance for an import client, but you suspect the invoice value has been inflated to facilitate money laundering. What red flags would you check, and what steps would you take?"

Nilesh: "Trade-based money laundering (TBML) is a serious compliance risk. I would check for:

- Invoice Overvaluation – Comparing declared values with market benchmarks
- Unusual Trade Routes – Multiple transit countries with no logical reason
- Shell Companies – Checking UBO (Ultimate Beneficial Ownership) details
- Mismatch in Documents – Discrepancies between commercial invoice, BL, and packing list
- Repeated Amendments in LCs – Frequent changes in terms can be a red flag

If suspicious activity is confirmed, I would:

- Report it to the bank's AML team & FIU-IND under PMLA guidelines.
- Seek additional KYC & transaction history before proceeding.
- Advise stricter trade financing structures, such as UCP600-compliant LCs, third-party audits, or dual confirmations.

Strict compliance with FATF, RBI, and FEMA guidelines is crucial to protect the bank from exposure to illicit activities."

Interviewer: "RBI has tightened the norms on capital account transactions under FEMA. How do these changes impact corporate outward remittances and ODI (Overseas Direct Investment)?"

Nilesh: "The recent changes impose stricter scrutiny on outward remittances under LRS (Liberalized Remittance Scheme) and ODI norms:

- Enhanced KYC and Due Diligence – Banks must now ensure that funds sent abroad are for genuine business purposes.
- Restricted Transactions – Certain investments in foreign startups and assets are now subject to RBI approval.
- Sector-Specific Limits – Industries like real estate, cryptocurrencies, and unregulated markets face tighter capital control measures.
- Increased Documentation Requirements – Proof of end-use, business viability, and regulatory approvals are now mandatory for ODI transactions.

These regulations ensure better forex reserves management and prevent capital flight, while still allowing genuine corporate expansion overseas."

Interviewer: "Nilesh, your responses have been insightful and demonstrate a deep understanding of forex, trade finance, risk management, and regulatory compliance. Given your leadership experience and analytical approach, I believe you are well-prepared for the AGM role.

Before we conclude, let me ask you one final question: Why do you believe you are the right fit for this promotion?"

Nilesh: "Thank you. I believe I am the right fit for this promotion because:

- Proven Business Growth – My ability to scale forex operations, credit portfolios, and branch profitability has been demonstrated at Madurai Main Branch.
- Strong Regulatory & Risk Management Acumen – I ensure compliance-first credit & forex solutions while optimizing business growth.
- Leadership & Team Development – I have successfully built high-performing teams that deliver results even in challenging market conditions.
- Data-Driven Decision Making – My structured approach ensures risk-mitigated lending, forex solutions, and trade finance strategies.
- Commitment to Overcoming Challenges – Despite my speech impairment, I have continuously refined my communication strategy, ensuring impactful leadership.

I am confident that my vision for corporate finance, forex expansion, and risk-controlled growth aligns with the bank's objectives for the AGM role. I look forward to contributing at a larger scale."

Interviewer: "Nilesh, thank you for this discussion. We appreciate your expertise and strategic thinking. We wish you all the best for the next stage.

Nilesh shakes hands with the panel, leaves the room with a composed confidence, knowing that he has given his best."

• • •

About The Author

Kumar Gaurav Khullar is a seasoned banker, trade finance expert, and banking mentor with a wealth of experience in the Banking and Finance sector. A former banker with Bank of India and Punjab & Sind Bank, he has held various roles across urban and rural branches, gaining hands-on expertise in General Banking, Credit/ Advances & Risk Management.

An accomplished academic, he holds an MBA from the prestigious Indian Institute of Management, Raipur (IIM-Raipur) and a Master's in Computer Applications (MCA) from the Centre for Development of Advanced Computing (CDAC-Noida). He is also a JAIIB & CAIIB certified professional from the Indian Institute of Banking and Finance, supplemented by specialized banking certifications from NIBSCOM (National Institute of Banking Studies & Corporate Management) & other premier financial institutions.

In 2018, he transitioned from banking services to teaching & content creation, driven by his mission to simplify complex banking concepts and make professional certifications more accessible to bankers. He has since helped thousands of banking and finance professionals prepare for and successfully clear JAIIB, CAIIB, Certified Credit Professional (CCP), and Anti-Money Laundering (AML) & Trade Finance exams.

A sought-after instructor, he offers best-selling courses on Udemy, including Basel Norms and Incoterms 2020 Masterclasses, with outstanding student feedback. He also runs the Bank Financial Management Case Studies course which is a unique case studies-based course for banking/ finance professionals

Additionally, he runs a thriving YouTube community of 55,000+ members, where he shares practical banking insights, career guidance, and survival strategies for banking professionals. His videos, such as "Factoring and Forfeiting Masterclass, Important Points Before Taking Charge of a New Branch", Ultimate Guide to Loan Proposals, Documentation and NPA Prevention for Bank Officers and Managers & "Save Your Banking Job – Vigilance 24/7", have helped countless bankers navigate real-world banking challenges.

With a mission to empower bankers with knowledge and confidence, Kumar Gaurav Khullar continues to bridge the gap between theory &

practical banking through his books, courses, and mentoring initiatives. His work is not just about clearing exams—it's about transforming careers and shaping the future of banking.

Contact me -
kumargauravkhullar1@gmail.com
+91-7830481000 (Whatsapp)

www.ingramcontent.com/pod-product-compliance
Lightning Source LLC
Chambersburg PA
CBHW041318120726
48005CB00014B/2047